POLAND

CHRISTIAN PARMA
photography

RENATA GRUNWALD-KOPEĆ
text

Wydawnictwo PARMA® PRESS

POLAND

Poland covers 312,679 km², making it the world's 69th largest country and Europe's 9th largest. Territorial waters extend over 8700 km², while the Vistula and Szczecin Lagoons cover 1200 km². The country's nearly 38.5 million inhabitants are 96% Polish, 4% ethnic minorities – mainly Germans, Belarusians and Ukrainians. The official language is Polish, the currency the złoty (of which 1 is made up of 100 groszy). The country is a pluralistic democracy with a parliament elected by universal suffrage every four years. 460 deputies sit in its Sejm or lower house, 100 senators in its Senat. The President of the Republic is in turn elected every 5 years. The legal foundations of the Third Republic of Poland are as set out in the Constitution of April 2nd 1997. The emblem of Poland is a white eagle in a golden crown facing right, with a golden beak and claws, set against a red rectangular field. The Polish colours are red and white and these are arranged horizontally on the country's flag, with white above and red below.

Administratively, Poland is divided into 16 voivodeships (province-regions), 379 poviats ("counties") plus 65 towns with poviat rights and 2479 urban, urban-rural, and rural gminas (local-authority areas). The nation's capital is Warsaw. The Polish calendar includes 13 public holidays, which are either national commemorations (Labour Day – May 1st, Constitution Day – May 3rd and Independence Day – November 11th) or days of religious significance (January 6th – Epiphany, two days at Easter, Whitsun, Corpus Christi, August 15th – the holiday of the Assumption of the Virgin Mary, November 1st – All Saints Day, December 25th and 26th – Christmas Day and Boxing Day), plus January 1st – New Year's Day.

THE HISTORY OF POLAND

Bolesław the Brave (967-1025)

Kazimierz the Great (1310-1370)

Zygmunt III Waza (1566-1632)

Władysław Jagiełło (1348-1434)

At the end of the first millennium A.D., a considerable part of Europe was inhabited by Slav tribes. The land that is now Poland belonged to the Western Slavs, including the Wiślanie (Vistulanian) tribe inhabiting the area around what is now Kraków, and the Polanie (Polanians) living around today's Gniezno. In the 10th century, the Polanians managed to unite some of the tribes under the ruling Piast family, and it was they who would go on to rule Poland for four centuries. In 966, one of their number – Duke Mieszko I – took baptism and initiated a new chapter in the history of Poland; whose full sovereignty as a country was confirmed during a meeting of Bolesław "the Brave" with Holy Roman Emperor Otto III held in Gniezno in the year 1000. Successive rulers gradually expanded Polish territory, incorporating it into the new Dukedom. However, a period of weakened statehood occurred after the 1138 death of Bolesław Krzywousty ("the Wrymouth"), whose last will assigned authority in each of five different parts of Poland to different Princes – his sons, with the most important deemed to be the one residing in Kraków. At the end of the 13th century and beginning of the 14th, Władysław Łokietek ("the Short") united the country once again. It was at this time that the power of the Teutonic Order of Knights of St. Mary the Virgin was growing in the north. Władysław the Short's successor, Kazimierz the Great, was nevertheless able to extend Polish territory still further, as well as promoting economic development and the increased significance of Poland in the international arena. The death of Kazimierz the Great in 1370 brought an end to the rule of the Piast dynasty. On the strength of agreements entered into previously with the Angevins, the throne of Poland was taken up by Louis of Hungary, and after his death in 1384 by Jadwiga. It was her marriage of the same year to Lithuanian King Władysław Jagiełło that started the Jagiellonian Dynasty of the nearly 200-year period 1386-1572. Under the King's command, the combined armies of Poland and Lithuania were successful in taking on the Teutonic Knights at the Battle of Grunwald in 1410. It was nevertheless to be some time later before the Knights received their final defeat – at the hands of Kazimierz IV Jagiellon, the ultimate victor of the Thirteen Years' War of 1454-1466. Further territory was gained in this way, and it was under the last of the Jagiellons – Zygmunt I "the Old", as well as Zygmunt II August – that Mazowsze (then Masovia) was added to Poland, while a peace agreement with Turkey was signed and the Parliament convened in Lublin in 1569 founded a Union between Poland and Lithuania known as the Commonwealth of the Two Nations. This was a strong state under one ruler, with a joint Parliament and foreign policy. Unsurprisingly, then, the 16th century is considered to have been a "golden age" for Poland. However, the death of Zygmunt August with no heir in 1572 ended the rule of the Jagiellons, leaving kingship a matter for elections by the nobility. There was to be no immediate successor to Zygmunt as one candidate for the Polish throne after another tried to win the support of electors by offering ever greater rights and privileges, and simultaneously eroding the rights and strength of the monarchy. The inevitable result as the elected Kings came and went was increasing chaos and enfeebled statehood. Most of the occupants of the throne from them on were not committed to a strengthened Poland, as they were not Poles and had no expectation that their descendants would accede to the throne after them. Moreover, the country was suffering depopulation and economic decline in the 17th century, as epidemics coincided with the onset of a long-lasting conflict with Sweden ultimately resulting in the invasion known as "The Deluge", with wars against Moscow and Turkey as well, and with threats to eastern parts from Cossack uprisings. It was thus in a splendid exception to an otherwise rather miserable rule of those times that Jan III Sobieski came to the throne in 1674. Under him, convincing and crucial victories were won over the Turks at Chocim in 1673 and Vienna ten years later. Sobieski died – in a Poland at peace – in 1696,

Jan III Sobieski (1624-1696)

"The Election of Stanisław August", by Bernardo Bellotto, alias Canaletto.

justifiably proud of his achievements and little suspecting that the approaching 18th century would in the main be an era of decline, as ever greater influence over Poland came to be exerted by its muscle-flexing imperial neighbours in Russia, Prussia and Austria. However, something of a valiant attempt to reverse this trend through renewed Polish statehood came with the 1764 election of King Stanisław August Poniatowski (who would in fact be Poland's last). Doubtless appreciating the threat posed to their authority, the neighbours engaged in the First Partition of (part of) Poland in 1772, provoking a patriotic response from the side of King and country, as the Commission on National Education was founded in 1773 and the Four-Year Sejm summoned in 1788. The culmination of this Parliament's activity was a magnificent, if doomed, gesture in the form of the enactment of the Constitution of May 3rd 1791 – the first of its kind in Europe and only the second in the world. The inevitable crackdown followed, with the Second Partition of 1793, followed by the Third and last of 1795 that ended Polish independence and erased the country from the map of Europe. King Stanisław was forced into abdication and exile. Polish armies arising subsequently – also in exile – played an active part in the wars prosecuted by France, counting on some kind of reward in the shape of Napoleon's support for their country's independence. In the event, the French defeat of the Prussians led to the creation of the Duchy of Warsaw in 1807. It was sadly to prove ephemeral as, with the French defeat in and retreat from Moscow, the Russian army poured into Warsaw in 1813. Two years later, the Congress of Vienna decided on the creation of a "Congress" Kingdom of Poland entirely subordinated to Russia. A number of uprisings or other forms of resistance against the three different occupying powers were to follow, but the chances were basically zero until all three of the

Partitioners found themselves on the losing side of World War I. The newly-independent Poland of 1918 slowly began to make up for more than 100 years deprived of its liberty. But the development of the economy, education, culture and art soon took on ever-greater dynamism, only for hopes to be dashed again so soon, as World War II broke out. Having to face aggression from both its eastern and western neighbours, Poland was probably World War II's greatest victim. The ruins it had been reduced to, and the millions of deaths it had suffered, by 1945, were worse than anything even its troubled history could recall. Worst of all, in the wake of such sacrifice, the status of Poland as one of the ultimately victorious allies (having fought on all fronts throughout) was not even rewarded by full post-War independence. Rather, the Teheran and Yalta Conferences of 1943 and 1945 agreed that Poland would fall "within the Soviet sphere of influence" – something which in fact meant complete submission to communist Moscow. This was a state of affairs that the Poles were to try and resist for years, proving ready to fight on for their democracy, and finally bringing about the 1980 establishment of the Solidarity trade union as a force opposing the communist authorities. Mass Solidarity-led protests from the public led to a state crackdown and the imposition of martial law on December 13th 1981. Only at the "Round Table" talks of 1989 did the authorities meet with representatives of the opposition. This was the death knell for communism, and a steady moved towards democracy followed. Solidarity leaders Lech Wałęsa and Tadeusz Mazowiecki being freely elected President and Prime Minister respectively. The return of national sovereignty led Poland to seek NATO membership, which it achieved on Marh 12th 1999. In turn, economic development and political will allowed the country to accede to the European Union on May 1st 2004.

POLAND'S GEOGRAPHY

Słowiński National Park and its wide, sandy beaches.

Poland is in Central Europe, but is also a Baltic Sea country, with its precise limits being set by meridians 14°07'E and 24°08'E, and parallels 49°00'N and 54°50'N. It covers 312,679 km². The latitudinal extent is sufficient to ensure that summer days on the coast are more than one hour longer than those in the mountains of the far south. The reverse situation applies in winter. Equally, the country extends far enough in the E-W direction to ensure a 40-minute difference in times of sunset and sunrise. Although in the Central European time zone, Eastern European time is adhered to in summer. The climate is temperate, though Poland lies within the transition zone between oceanic and continental influences. As a consequence, the weather is variable from season to season and from year to year. Today's Poland has seven neighbours: Germany to the west, the Czech Republic and Slovakia to the south, Ukraine, Belarus and Lithuania to the east and Russia's Kaliningrad District to the north. There are also 528 km of Baltic shoreline. The country's capital, Warsaw (Warszawa) has 1,700,000 people and is not far from the geometric centre of Europe. In geomorphological terms, Poland finds itself at the meeting point of three large tectonic units, namely: the Eastern European Pre-Cambrian Platform, the Central and Western European Palaeozoic Platform and the Alpids Orogen (mountain formation). Poland is nevertheless a prevalently lowland country, with more than 91% of its area below 300 m a.s.l., and an average altitude of just 173 m (cf. a European average of 330 m). The lowest point is in the Vistula Delta area near Raczki Elbląskie (at 1.8 m below sea level), while the highest is the 2499 m south-western peak of Mt. Rysy in the High Tatras. The relief and landscape of the country are thus varied, with the southern mountain belt of varying height, geological structure and age giving way to the north to an extensive upland, then a central plain as flat as a pancake, a series of picturesque lakelands, forests and marshes some way in from the coast and the coastal belt itself. Rivers thus range from fast-flowing mountain brooks to lazily meandering lowland rivers both big and small.

So, the southern border with Slovakia is formed by the Western Carpathians (peaking in the High and Western Tatra ranges). North of this is the Podhale Basin, and beyond it a further range collectively called the Beskids, and including the Western Beskids (as divided into the High and Low ranges), as well as the Eastern Beskids and Bieszczady Mountains, stretching beyond the Łupkowska Pass to the meeting point of the Polish, Slovakian and Ukrainian borders. In general, the Beskids have rounded tops and numerous valleys. Extending to the north of them is the Carpathian Foreland and beyond that (as separated by the Sandomierz and Oświęcim Basins) is a further belt of uplands and old mountains, separated by depressions and called – from west to east – the Silesian Upland, the Małopolska Upland (comprising the Kraków-Częstochowa Upland, Wośniki-Wieluń Upland, the Nida Syncline, the Kielce-Sandomierz Upland and Świętokrzyskie Mountains) and the Lublin Upland and Roztocze. The highest of these ranges are the Świętokrzyskie ("Holy Cross") Mountains, Palaeozoic in origin, with their characteristic upper parts including quartzite screes. The south west of the country bordering with the Czech Republic also boasts the Sudety range – Poland's second highest mountains. These comprise many sub-ranges, including – on the Polish side – the Kaczawskie and Sowie Mountains, and parts of the Izerskie, Karkonosze, Stołowe, Bystrzyckie and Złote Mountains. The Karkonosze (peaking at 1602 m Śnieżka) form the highest and best-known range. North of the Sudety there begins the belt of Central Polish Lowlands extending all the way to the eastern border, and contiguous with plains of a similar kind going all the way to the Urals. Included within the Polish part are the Silesian, Wielkopolska, Mazowsze (Mazovian), Podlasie and Polesie-Lublin Plains, with their peaceful rustic landscapes. North of the plains, and again extending across the whole country and beyond is a lakeland belt. This comprises the Wielkopolska and Pomeranian Lakelands west of the River Vistula, as well as the famous Mazurian Lakeland to the east. The lakes lie in the depressions between relatively high elevations, with the entire landscape having been "bulldozed" into this kind of shape by the ice sheets of the last Ice Age. The Mazurian Lakeland has the greatest number of lakes, and the biggest. The Baltic Coast in turn features a lowland plain with two particular depressions where the Rivers Odra (Oder) and Wisła (Vistula) meander down to the sea. However, while most of the shore is flat and sandy, with spits, lagoons and dunes, there are stretches of steep and relatively high cliffs, being continually regenerated by the cutting action of the waves below. 99.7% of Poland is within the Baltic Sea basin, with 55.7% being drained by the Vistula (the country's largest river) and 33.9% by the Oder. 9.3% of the country is drained by rivers feeding directly into the Baltic, 0.8% is within the basin of the Neman, while rain falling in just 0.3% of the far south-west or far south-east respectively will ultimately make its way to the Black and North Seas. The river network is diverse – densest in the Carpathian and Sudety Mountains on account of the high rainfall, rather impermeable substratum and diversified relief. Poland has around 9300 lakes covering more than 1 ha, most in the aforementioned lakelands. The deepest lakes are lowland Lakes Hańcza (108.5 m) and Drawsko (79.9 m), and Wielki Staw Polski in the Tatras (79.3 m). L. Śniardwy covers the largest area (109.7 km^2). The Polish tradition in the conservation of nature extends back to the Middle Ages. As early as in the 11th century, Bolesław Chrobry ordered restrictions on the trapping of beavers, while Kazimierz the Great (in 1347) and Władysław Jagiełło (in 1423) introduced bans on the cutting of old oaks and yews. In 1868 the Parliament in Lvov issued an act of law – the first of its kind in the world – bringing mountain fauna (chamois and marmots) under protection. The Poland of today boasts no fewer than 23 National Parks, among which 9 feature on the UNESCO world list of Biosphere Reserves. More than 120 Landscape Parks have been established, and nearly 1500 Nature Reserves. More than 70 different mineral resources are exploited, 40% involves the working of hard coal, 35% sand and gravel, 8% each brown coal and limestone, and the remainder sulphur, rock salt, copper ore, iron ore, zinc, lead, nickel, barite and silver. Also of major economic significance are Poland's granites, marbles and sandstones. The country also has a wealth of waters of geothermal value, and hot springs that have favoured spa treatment with waters containing chlorides, bicarbonates and sulphurous compounds.

The Suwałki region – a post-glacial landscape.

Mazowsze – a land of plains.

The Eastern Beskids. The Bieszczady Mountain landscape.

The Tatra Mountains and their high-mountain landscape.

1 ZACHODNIOPOMORSKIE
VOIVODESHIP (WESTERN POMERANIA)

Capital: **SZCZECIN**

Situated in the north west and taking in a large part of the region known for a century as Western Pomerania, it covers almost 30,000 km². To the west lies Germany, to the north the Baltic shore. The area retains traces of the various spheres of influence it has come under down the centuries: of Polish and German rulers, those of Denmark and Brandenburg; in the 17th century it came under Swedish rule, but a hundred years later it was German. Only after the Second World War did this part of Europe come once again within the territorial limits of Poland. The seat of the voivodeship is Szczecin – a city with a history stretching back to the 7th century, that is this region's chief industrial centre, complete with port and shipyard. Tourists are drawn here by the proximity of the sea, as well as the presence of old architecture (including that qualifying Szczecin as a stop along the European Route of Brick Gothic. The effect is only enhanced by the city's location between three large forest complexes.

Characteristic elements along the seashore in this area are steep cliffs – very high in places and constantly being cut away by the waves. The Baltic claims about 80 cm a year on

Szczecin, a city on the Szczecin Lagoon and commercial port. Its Old Market Square features colourful restored tenement houses.

Szczecin. The Renaissance castle of the Dukes of Pomerania is multi-winged, with two courtyards. It was rebuilt post-1945.

Szczecin. September 2014 brought the opening of the new Philharmonic Hall.

Międzyzdroje, a seaside holiday and health resort.

average, and, although the cliffs are reinforced in many places, nature is merciless and has time on her side. If you don't believe it, go and see what is left of the 15th-century church in Trzęsacz, once 1800 metres inland – all but one wall has now crashed down the cliff into the sea beneath. The region also has in excess of 1000 lakes, several tens of rivers and the fine Goleniów, Wkrzańska, Barlinek, Drawsko and Myśliwskie Forests. The two National Parks include that occupying the most interesting, greater part of Wolin island. An attraction for the visitor there is the European Bison Show Reserve.

Wolin is a town on the island of the same name, by the Szczecin Lagoon. From 1993 onwards, this has played host to the international Festival of Slavs and Vikings, which takes place between July and August.

Dziwnów is a large seaside resort, but also a fishing port. Fishermen are seen here sorting and spreading their nets.

Kamień Pomorski is an old port town with a historic urban layout. Seen here in all its finesse, the decorative southern elevation of the town's Gothic-style Cathedral.

Tuczno, a city founded in the early 14th century, was formerly the property of the Wedel family. The Mediaeval castle was rebuilt in the Renaissance and Baroque periods.

Dziwnówek, another sunset over the Baltic.

Drawieński National Park in turn includes Lake Drawsko – Poland's second deepest at up to 79.9 m. The bunkers of the Pomeranian Fortifications remain in place not far away. Both National Parks feature rare wildlife like white-tailed eagles, ospreys, otters and beavers. Another treat for nature-lovers at migration time are Poland's largest congregations of cranes, to be seen near Ińsko. The best-known holiday resorts in the area are: Darłowo, Dąbki, Mielno, Sarbinowo, Ustronie Morskie, Dźwirzyno, Mrzeżyno, Niechorze, Rewal and Kamień

Krąg, a holiday village with a 16th-century castle restored in the late 20th century by a private investor.

Pniewo. The idiosyncratic "Crooked Forest" with unnaturally crooked tree trunks; the cause of this deformation remains unexplained.

Brzesko, a village of medieval provenance with the Sanctuary of the Brzesko Virgin Mary. The church features polychrome wooden stalactite vaulting.

Pomorski. In turn, at the health resorts like Świnoujście, Międzyzdroje, Kołobrzeg and Połczyn-Zdrój, you can take a cure in the form of deposits of therapeutic muds and healing spring waters. Many localities retain at least some features of earlier architecture – castles, palaces, and churches, parts of town walls with towers and gates, and old tenement houses. Darłowo features: a castle of the Dukes of Pomerania erected between the 14th and 17th centuries, and the Gothic St. Mary's Church dating back to 1394, and often remodelled subsequently. In Koszalin, the visitor's attention is drawn to the Gothic-style Church of the Virgin Mary with its

Kołbacz. The Gothic Cistercian Abbey complex from the 13th-15th centuries.

Słutowo features the Late-Gothic Church of the Lord's Transfiguration, erected using stone in the late 15th and early 16th centuries (and hence not typical at all).

imposing tower. Inside it plays host to many valuable works of art. Move east of Koszalin and Krąg is seen to contain a rather unusual castle with 4 towers, 12 entrances, 52 rooms and 365 windows. Biały Bór in turn retains innocent-looking tenement houses that are actually the upper parts of huge bunkers. Other interesting monuments can be seen in Białogard, Trzebiatów (the palace complex), Gryfice, Kamień Pomorski, Płoty, Nowogard, Stargard, Świdwin, Tuczno and Połczyn-Zdrój.

Świdwin. Castle of the Teutonic Knights built on the site of a former Slavic settlement.

Stargard was a Pomeranian defensive settlement that won its town charter as long ago as in 1243. The town walls and gates survive, along with the Gothic collegiate church whose interiors feature bricks of various different colours.

Chojna is a town founded in the 13th century and featuring many heritage items along the "European Route of Brick Gothic Architecture" – not least the 15th-century Świecie Gate (named after the nearby centre).

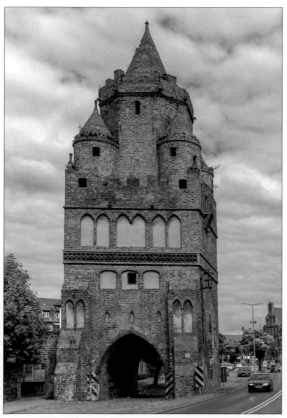

2 POMORSKIE
VOIVODESHIP (POMERANIA)

Capital: **GDAŃSK**

This 18,000 km² part of Pomerania, sometimes termed Gdańsk Pomerania, was within Poland up to the 12th century, before becoming an independent dukedom until the 14th century, when it was taken by the Teutonic Knights. The second half of the 15th century brought a return to Poland maintained to the time of the Partitions, when the area passed to Prussia. In 1919 it became Polish again, though Gdańsk itself retained Free City status (as Danzig). At 4.45 on September 1st 1939, the German bombardment of the nearby Westerplatte peninsula launched World War II.

Gdańsk is joined by Sopot and Gdynia in creating what is known as the Trójmiasto ("Tri-City") – an urban complex covering some 415 km². Gdańsk can boast more than 1000 years of history and has a great deal of fine heritage architecture. Tourists come in their millions to see St. Mary's Basilica, the Cathedral in Oliwa district, the Neptune Fountain and the Old Port Crane; as well as to be able to take a walk through the picturesque streets of the wider Old Town area. The city also has the world's leading concentration

Gdańsk. The Great Council Chamber in the Town Hall of Gdańsk Main Town, also known as the Red Room. The impressive Mannerist-style ceiling features a plafond painted by Izaak van den Blocke and entitled "The Apotheosis of Gdańsk".

Gdańsk is a historic port city once within the Hanseatic League. Here part of the Main Town with the Church of Saints Mary and Nicholas, the Market Hall and Jacek Tower, all as seen from the tower of St. Elizabeth's Church.

Gdańsk. The Neptune Fountain on Długi Targ (the Long Market).

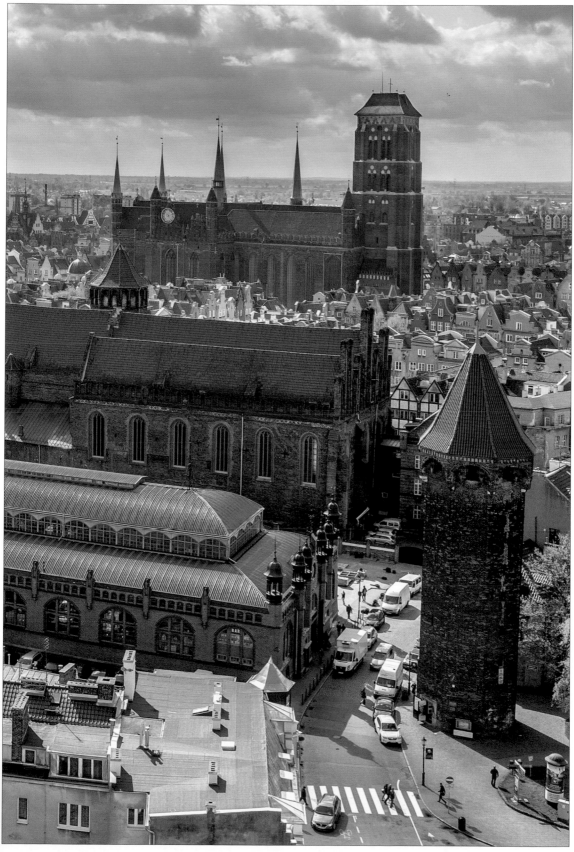

Gdynia as a city has only existed since 1926 – four years after the Polish Sejm enacted a Bill providing for the construction of this new Baltic port. Here the Southern Pier, with a view across to the Sea Towers.

Gdańsk, Westerplatte – a monument to those who fell at the very start of the Second World War was erected here in 1945.

Sopot is Poland's best-known seaside resort. The Dom Zdrojowy in the Haffner Centre was given over for use in 2009. It is by the beach, and very close to the famous pier.

of workshops and shops serving the trade in amber.

The adjacent Sopot formed a "Riviera of the North" in the late 19th and early 20th centuries, being an elegant and fashionable resort also famous for its casinos and horse racing. It still boasts Europe's longest wooden pier, as well as the Forest Opera that plays host each year to the city's International Song Festival.

Gdynia is one the country's youngest cities, becoming the most modern and largest Baltic port just prior to WWII. Floating museums worth a visit include the "Dar Pomorza" sailing

Each year brings a Fishermen's Sea Pilgrimage, which ends with a Mass celebrated at the Church of the Holy Apostles Peter and Paul in Puck.

Słowiński National Park, by the Baltic shore, was founded in 1967. Here a storm has uncovered remnants of a forest present 3000 years ago, probably burnt, then covered in blown sand, before being inundated by the sea.

ship and the Polish Navy's "Błyskawica", both in the Northern Harbour area.

The largest centre in the western part of the voivodeship is Słupsk, whose monuments to past history include the castle of the Dukes of Pomerania, parts of the defensive walls, the city gates, a castle mill, churches and tenement houses.

One of the most precious monuments of defensive architecture, entered on UNESCO's World Heritage List, is the Castle in Malbork, the former capital of the Teutonic Knights. Also dating back to this era are the castles in Gniew, Bytów, Kwidzyn and Człuchów.

Of particular note is the former Cistercian Monastery complex in Pelplin, which dates back to the 13th and 14th centuries. Among the elements characterizing the Gothic

Pelplin. The Cathedral of the Blessed Virgin Mary is part of an old Cistercian Abbey complex.

Kartuzy. The interior of the Gothic-Baroque Church of the Assumption is of stone and brick.

appearance restored in the 19th century are interesting Gothic and Renaissance style stalls, as well as fine frescoes in the cloisters. Pomerania pleases tourists with its beautiful beaches, plentiful lakes and forests. There are two National Parks (also now listed as Biosphere Reserves) – Słowiński in the north, renowned for its mobile dunes up to 30 m high and the Bory Tucholskie (Tuchola Forest) NP in the south.

The Pomeranian part of the Baltic coast resembles the Western Pomeranian in being varied. There are both cliffs and wide, sandy beaches, and dunes, forests, spits and lagoon-lakes behind sandbars (like Łebsko, Gardno

Chojnice is a town on the edge of the Tuchola Forest. The market square features this Neo-Gothic Town Hall.

Malbork. The castle, which was the seat of the Teutonic Order's Grand Masters, dates back to the 13th-15th centuries, and is one of the finest surviving examples of a Mediaeval fortress.

Malbork. The Convent Chamber in the High Castle. In the Middle Ages this was a place of repose, first and foremost following dinner.

Kiezmark is a Żuławy-region village featuring the 18th-century Church of the Częstochowa Mother of God, which is in part of wattle-and-daub construction.

Tczew is one of Pomerania's oldest towns, and is in the Kociewie area. The road (initially road-and-rail) bridge over the Vistula was built in the mid-19th century.

Gniew. Overlooking the Vistula is a 14th-century castle of the Teutonic Knights that was built in the shape of a regular square.

and Sarbsko). The most popular coastal resorts are Ustka, Rowy, Łeba, Jastrzębia Góra, Władysławowo and Puck, as well as Jastarnia and Krynica Morska sited on the Hel and Vistula Spits respectively. Inland, tourists seek rest and recreation around the lakes in Charzykowo, Chmielno, Przywidz and Wdzydze Kiszewskie, or else obtain a closer look on canoe trips.

Kwidzyn has a brick-built Gothic cathedral complex devoted to the Virgin Mary and St. John the Envangelist, as well as a castle with square courtyard.

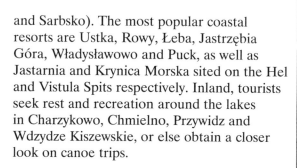
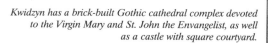

3 KUJAWSKO-POMORSKIE
VOIVODESHIP (KUJAWY-POMERANIA)

Capital: **BYDGOSZCZ**

This voivodeship takes in the Kujawy region itself (historically Kuyavia), and part of Pomerania, as well as the Dobrzyń land and areas historically associated with Wielkopolska. The capital is Bydgoszcz on the Rivers Brda and Vistula. Its development, beginning from the 14th century, was based mainly on the salt and cereal trades. The best-known buildings are the Late Gothic Church in the Old Town and the three old grain stores by the Brda. An equally important city in the province is Toruń, which is entered on UNESCO's World Heritage List on account of its preserved Mediaeval town plan in the Old Town area. A further centre in the voivodeship is Włocławek, which is renowned for the beautiful ceramics produced there. In turn, Grudziądz also retains a Mediaeval town plan and monuments of its own – above all a complex of 26 granaries erected between the 14th and 17th centuries on the escarpment above the Vistula.

The best-preserved and known castle in this area is the one in Golub-Dobrzyń. Knight tournaments of international rank take place here, and the castle of the Teutonic Knights in the village of Zamek Bierzgłowski remains

Bydgoszcz stands on the Brda and the Bydgoszcz Canal. This was a centre of the salt trade in the 15th and 16th centuries. Seen here are the riverside boulevards, as well as sculptures from the 2004 open-air exhibition.

In Bydgoszcz, the Statue of the Archer in Kochanowski Park. This is one of the city's oldest statues, unveiled in 1910.

in a fairly good state. In contrast, in Radzyń Chełmiński, Świecie and Wenecja the castles have been reduced to ruins. In Kruszwica, there is a tower known as Mysia, in which a legendary King Popiel is said to have been eaten by mice, thereby leaving the throne available for Poland's first dynasty of Christian Kings, the Piasts. Beautiful heritage architecture can also be seen in Lubostroń, Jabłonów Pomorski, Brodnica, Chełmno (sourrounded still by its old defensive walls), Mogilno, Skępe, Strzelno (with its

Bydgoszcz. The Old Market Square with the Town Hall and the tower of the Cathedral of Saint Martin and St. Nicholas. And, in the foreground, the Monument to Struggle and Martyrdom in the Bydgoszcz Region.

Toruń. Here we see the monument to the city's most famous son, Nicholas Copernicus, against the buckground of the Gothic-style Town Hall.

Toruń is one of Poland's oldest urban centres, which was once a member of the Hanseatic League. Here the view of the Old Town by the Vistula, with the defensive ramparts, built-up area, Church of the Holy Ghost and Cathedral of the Saints John.

Strzelno. One of seven Romanesque columns in the Church of the Holy Trinity and the Blessed Virgin Mary, decorated with figural and ornamental bas-reliefs.

Biskupin. A reconstruction of the pre-Slavic settlement with defensive ramparts and houses.

Romanesque rotunda of St. Procopius), Chełmża, Włocławek and many other places. Biskupin is a worth a visit, boasting a reconstruction of a pre-Slavic settlement from the Halstadtian period (550-400 B.C.). The site hosts archaeological festivals at which the visitor may really see how everyday life in those far off times must have looked. Many other places in the voivodęship give testimony to the very early settlement of the area: the village of Wietrzychowice has megalithic burial grounds 4000 years old, while the oldest exhibits at the museum in Kruszwica data back more than 4500 years Natural resources of the Kujawy area include

Lubostroń is the village that Count Fryderyk Skórzewski selected for the construction of his family palace in the years 1795-1800. Here, one of its interiors, adorned by a mural that is the work of the Smuglewicz Brothers.

Inowrocław is now known mainly as a health resort, though rock salt was also mined here until recently. This (reconstructed) Romanesque church was originally from the 12th-13th centuries.

its deposits of salt. Research has shown that this was already being worked two centuries B.C. At Ciechocinek and Inowrocław, salty waters have been used as spa cures – for respiratory complaints among other things – for more than 150 years. The wooden structures wherein such waters are converted into fine sprays and inhaled are from the 19th century and the complex is the biggest of its kind in the world.

The most popular holiday centres in this region are Koronowo, Brodnica, Tuchola, Bachotek, the Chełmża area, Kruszwica and Biskupin. There are Landscape Parks and a number of nature reserves, as well as several massive oaks: one in Nogat has a trunk of

Ciechocinek has been a place to spa waters since the 19th century. Here, the wooden building in which salty vapours can be inhaled.

Sunset over Lake Sumińskie in the Dobrzyń Lakeland.

circumference 940 cm, while another in Bąkowo has almost as great a girth, of 890 cm. In turn, within the Tuchola Forest, near Osłuchowo, stands another monument of nature, St. Adalbert's Stone. This glacial erratic (boulder carried by ice sheets and dropped when they melted) has a circumference of 24.5 m and a height of 3.5 m.

Świecie. This town by the Vistula is of Mediaeval origin. It is famous for its mid-14th-century Gothic-style Castle of the Teutonic Knights, among other things.

Chełmno is a town by the Vistula retaining its original grid street-plan, its walls and gates and towers, as well as a Renaissance-era Town Hall with a very tall and decorative attic.

Grudziądz is a very old town, first mentioned in 1064. Here the view from Zamkowa ("Castle") Street, of buildings in the Old Town's Spichrzowa Street.

Radzyń Chełmiński obtained its town rights at the beginning
of the 13th century. The castle of the Commander of the Order of
Teutonic Knights built in Gothic style less than a century later is
among the largest in the State the Order ran at that time.

Brodnica. A heritage-rich small town on the edge
of the Brodnica Lakeland. This Gothic tower is what
remains of the old castle of the Teutonic Knights.

Golub-Dobrzyń boasts a 14th-century castle remodelled
in Renaissance style in the 1600s. Each year, this plays host
to tournaments of jousting and other chivalrous skills.

Capital: **OLSZTYN**

The voivodeship includes two picturesque lands from history, i.e. Varmia and Mazuria. It is known even more colourfully as the "Land of the Thousand Lakes" and has only around 1.5 million people across its 24,000 km². Varmia was originally inhabited by a Prussian tribe of a similar name, as one of the Balt peoples settled from the middle of the first millennium A.D. in the land between the mouths of the Vistula and Neman. Later, and particularly during the region's occupation by the Teutonic Knights, the people became Germanised and annihilated. Mazuria also belonged to the Prussians in the early Middle Ages, though it was colonized by Poles from neighbouring Mazovia from the 14th century on. Today's Varmia-Mazury is home to many cultures – the core population of inhabitants whose ancestors settled here long ago, plus those of Polish and Ukrainian origin, Lemko people and the descendents of Germans. There are Catholics and Evangelical Protestants, as well as followers of the Byzantine-Ukrainian church.

The voivodeship capital is Olsztyn, a city founded in the 14th century by the Teutonic

Olsztyn. Freedom Square (Plac Wolności) with its early 20th-century Town Hall built in a style that recalls the Baroque and Renaissance periods.

Olsztyn on the River Łyna and within the Olsztyn Lakeland. This reconstructed 14th-century castle was that of the Varmia Chapter.

Nowe Kawkowo is a village not far from Olsztyn. Its lavender fields, which are most likely Poland's largest, have become a tourist attraction in their own right.

Łukta is a large village in the Masuria region which boasts an interesting Gothic-style church (with later tower). The Knights of the Teutonic Order had this built in 1407.

Knights. The astronomer Copernicus was active here as an administrator of the Varmia Chapter in the 16th century. The astronomer lived in the castle of the aforementioned Chapter which still stands today as the present seat of the Museum of Varmia and Mazury. The tradition of interest in the cosmos continues at the Olsztyn Planetarium. The second most important city in the region is Elbląg, which obtained its charter as early as in the 13th century, at which time it was the seat of the Teutonic Knights and a member of the Hanseatic League. It had a large port, and Poland's first shipyard from

Ostróda. The Gothic castle of the Teutonic Knights was entirely rebuilt in the 1970s.

27

The Iławd Lakeland was once known as Western Masuria. There is a large amount of land under forest here, as well as the obvious lakes, and all of this ensures a status as of interest to tourists.

Grunwald. Knights of today fight on the site of the famous victory over the Teutonic Knights of 1410.

1570 onwards. The partition of 1772 left it in Prussian hands, and it did not return to Poland until after World War II. The voivodeship's many heritage buildings include the fortified cathedral in Frombork, the collegiate church in Dobre Miasto, the castles built by the Teutonic Knights in Kętrzyn, Nidzica and Ostróda, the castle of the Bishops of Varmia in Reszel, the Bishops' castles in Szymbark and Lidzbark Warmiński, and the churches in Święta Lipka, Braniewo, Elbląg, Olsztyn and Kętrzyn. At Grunwald, the 1410 victory of Poland and Lithuania over the Teutonic Knights that happened here is commemorated at a Monument to the event.

Grunwald. Visible from afar on its mound is the Monument to the Victory and Grunwald.

Nidzica is a town on the River Nida. It has yet-another well-
preserved 14th-century castle of the Teutonic Knights. To be seen
here is the south-eastern tower and defensive moat.

The Town Hall in Morąg dates back to the late 14th century,
and is one of Poland's very few surviving items of secular
Gothic architecture.

The Elbląg Canal was built in the mid-19th century,
to make transport by water to and from the Baltic possible.
The construction is 151 km long overall, and currently represents
a major tourist attraction for the region. At Jelenie, boats are
lifted up a canal inclined plane.

Elbląg gained its town rights in 1246, but was much destroyed
during World War II. Rebuilding work on the Old Town began
at the end of the 20th century. Here the 15th-century Market Gate,
as well as new tenement houses on the Old Market Square.

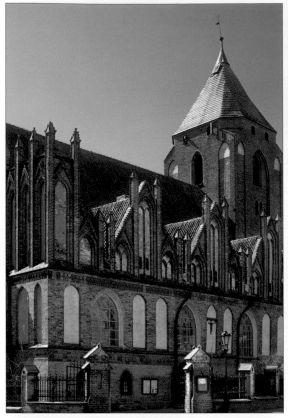

Frombork. The Madonna and Child forms the central part of a Late-Gothic altar polyptych in the Cathedral, which is regarded as the most beautiful place of worship anywhere in Warmia (Varmia).

Orneta. This Warmia town founded in the 14th century has plenty of heritage architecture. Here (the northern elevation of) its Gothic-style Church of St. John the Baptist and St. John the Evangelist.

Reszel. In this small Warmia town there is a Bishop's Castle dating back to the mid-14th century. The 19th century in turn brought a conversion of its northern wing into a church.

A further major attraction of the region is the 19th-century Elbląg Canal, with its locks, inclines and aqueduct passing over the surface of a lake. In turn, the region's forests retain ruins of German bunkers from World War II: the most famous of all, Hitler's former HQ near Gierłoż, as well as the Wehrmacht headquarters in Mamerki. Varmia-Mazury is above all a tourist region. Apart from in Olsztyn and Elbląg there is no heavy industry to speak of here, and so this is the cleanest part of Poland. It boasts several

Lidzbark Warmiński. Castle of the Bishops of Varmia, built of brick in the Gothic style.

Stoczek Klasztorny. This boasts a Warmia-region Sanctuary for the Virgin Mary as Queen of Peace. Depicted are the cloisters of the formerly Bernardine Monastery currently belonging to the Congregation of Marian Fathers of the Immaculate Conception.

Święta Lipka boasts a Baroque Jesuit monastery complex with the Church of the Visitation. The interior of the latter has a famous organ with moving decorative elements.

Landscape Parks and a great many Nature Reserves, in which rare species of fauna and flora enjoy protection. It is also the perfect place for tourism based around water, with the shores of lakes boasting many jetties, harbours and watersports centres (including those for winter sports). Trips by canoe and passenger cruises are organized, while the forests on the lakeshores support holiday centres and camping sites. The greatest numbers of tourists choose to holiday around Giżycko, Mikołajki, Ruciane-Nida, Mrągowo, Morąg, Iława, Gołdap, Olsztyn, Olsztynek and Ostróda.

The Borecka Forest is a large forest complex in the Ełk Lakeland.

5 PODLASKIE
VOIVODESHIP (PODLASIE)

Capital: **BIAŁYSTOK**

Situated in the north-eastern corner of Poland, this voivodeship includes the Suwałki region and part of what was historically Podlasie. It borders to the east with Lithuania and Belarus, and retains several different cultures – of Poles, Belarusians, Lithuanians, and the descendents of Tartars settling in several villages here as long ago as in the times of Jan III Sobieski. To this day, Catholics, Orthodox worshippers and Moslems live side by side in this region. The capital of the region is Białystok, with 280,000 people. Other more important towns in the region include Łomża, Suwałki, Augustów, Wysokie Mazowieckie and Grajewo. Podlasie voivodeship is a little-industrialised part of the country, with a wealth of unspoilt nature, wild forests and unregulated rivers (like the world-famous Biebrza). Much of it is covered in forest, and this sometimes forms large complexes of a primaeval character. Examples here are the world-famous Białowieża Forest, as well as those in the Augustów and Knyszyn areas, and the so-called Czerwony Bór ("Red Forest"). The Białowieża Forest is a World Heritage Site. More generally, no less than 40% of the province enjoys legal protection and there are

Białystok. The interior of the Baroque place of the Branicki family. The Medical Scool's
"Aula Magna" brasts rich stucco-work, paintings and tapestries.

Białystok, on the River Biała, was founded in the 15th century. A view of the Parish Church of the Assumption comprising a bijou Baroque-style church (on to which a Neo-Gothic archicathedral was later built).

Białystok. A post-War reconstruction is the Baroque Town Hall now housing the District Museum.

Kruszyniany. The doors of the Tartar Mosque. The elevation's green colour is not there by chance, for green is the colour of Islam.

four National Parks: Białowieski (containing the aforementioned Białowieża Forest), Narwiański along the River Narew, Biebrzański along the Biebrza and Wigierski around the large Lake Wigry. These areas are augmented by the Suwałki, Łomża, Bug River and Knyszyn Forest Landscape Parks and more than 80 Nature Reserves. Beavers, wolves, lynxes and European bison can all be found here, the latter the pride of the region and whole country. The 300 lakes in the region include Hańcza, Poland's deepest. Navigation is rather well developed, and the conditions are fine for waterborne tourism,

Tykocin. The interior of the Baroque synagogue is now a museum to Judaism.

33

Wigry. The formerly Calmeldolite monastery complex with its Baroque-style Church of the Immaculate Conception, situated by Lake Wigry.

Sejny is a town in the Suwałki Lakeland. The Basilica of the Visitation is the Sanctuary for the Sejny Mother of God, and forms part of a Dominican Monastery complex.

A Lock Paniewo on the Augustów Canal, between Lakes Białe and Studziennicze.

especially by canoe. A waterway of heritage significance is the Augustów Canal dating back to the first half of the 19th century and linking the Vistula and Neman Basins. The Canal is 102 km long, has 18 stone locks and can carry vessels of up to 100 tonnes. A good break away from it all can be taken in Augustów itself, by L. Wigry, or in the Suwałki and Siemianówka areas. There are plenty of architecturally-valuable structures to take in too, notably: the manor of the Lutosławski family in Drozdowo, the church and monastery complex by Lake Wigry, and the churches in Sejny, Drohiczyn and Siemiatycze. The region includes a number

Stańczyki. Dating back to the early 20th century, a never-finished railway viaduct contrasts with the landscape in the Suwałki region, a famously picturesque one of postglacial relief and landforms, as well as a wealth of nature.

Nowogród. The Kurpie Region Outdoor Museum opened as long ago as in 1927. Currently covering more than 3 ha, it has down the years brought together residential and farm buildings, old chapels and shrines, as well as a wide variety farm implements.

Rajgród. The Neo-Gothic Church of the Nativity – dating from the early 20th century. This is a Sanctuary of the Rajgród Mother of God, of which the 17th-century likeness is to be seen in the Main Altar.

Łomża had town rights from the 14th century onwards – here a tenement house from the late 19th and early 20th centuries holds courtrooms.

Wizna is a village situated on the River Narew. The Church of St. John the Baptist has a squat shape, decorative upper parts and small windows – all typical distinguishing features of the so-called Masovian Gothic style.

*The Biebrza Marshes in Biebrzański National Park
– a natural area unique in Europe.*

*The Osowiec Fortress was built at the end of the 19th century by
the Tsarist authorities. It guards a key route across the Biebrza
Marshes.*

of churches and sacred sites for the Russian Orthodox Church, e.g. large numbers of churches in places such as Bielsk Podlaski, Białowieża, Mielnik, Sokółka, Białystok and Hajnówka, as well as the Święta Góra Grabarka site, with its forest of crosses of penitence brought here by the faithful. Those following the old ritual have their places of worship, known as molenny in Wodziłki and Gabowe Grądy. Moslems continue to pray at the mosques in Kruszyniany and Bohoniki; with the former also boasting a Moslem cemetery. It is also worth remembering about the museum of Judaism in the old synagogue in Tykocin, the museums of natural history in Białowieża and Drozdowo, and the open-air museums in Ciechanowiec, Nowogród and Jurowce.

*Ciechanowiec. The display of old steam-powered
machinery at the open-air museum.*

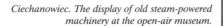

Drohiczyn was the historical capital of the Podlasie region. Here the gorge through which the Bug flows, as seen from Castle Hill.

Grabarka has its "Holy Hill", as Poland's most famous Sanctuary of the Orthodox Church. The faithful pray here among crosses brought by pilgrims down the generations.

Hajnówka is a town on the edge of Białowieża Forest. A performance is given by an Orthodox choir in Holy Trinity Church. The polychromy and iconostasy is the 1987 work of Greek artist Dymitrios Andonopulas.

Bielsk Podlaski is a town located on the River Biała. The Orthodox Parish Church of the Lord's Resurrection is one of the town's six.

Budy is a village in the renowned Białowieża Primaeval Forest; in this open-air museum, the interior of a 19th-century cottage that represents the so-called hutorowy type of settlement.

Białowieża. The 1845 manor house here was a stables for the Tsar's entourage. Today it serves as the National Park's Nature Education Centre.

Białowieża. The European bison – the biggest tourist attraction.

Puszcza Białowieska is a large complex of forest with primaeval features which also continues beyond the border with Belarus. Long a National Park, the Forest also enjoys both World Heritage Site and Biosphere Reserve status.

6 MAZOWIECKIE
VOIVODESHIP (MAZOWSZE)

Capital: **WARSAW**

Covering 35,000 km², Mazowsze is the largest of the voivodeships. It also has the largest population – in excess of 5 million. Most of it coincides with the historical Mazowsze (formerly known as Mazovia or Masovia), which was already within Poland by the period of the 10th-12th centuries. It was in an independent dukedom for a long time subsequently, however, though it was reincorporated into Poland bit by bit so that all was back within the fold by the first half of the 16th century (following the death of the last Duke of Mazovia without issue). Warsaw has been the region's capital since the early 17th century. The partitions saw Mazowsze carved up between the Prussian and Austrians,

though at the time of the Napoleonic Wars (1807-1815) it became the Duchy of Warsaw under the French, as it were, and then with their defeat at the hands of the Russians the Congress Kingdom of Poland, little more than a vassal of Moscow. And this is what it stayed until Poland came back on to the map of Europe at the end of World War I.

Warsaw is the largest centre of the voivodeship in terms of industry, culture and tourism. This was a market and defensive township as early as in the 10th century, but only officially a town from the mid 13th on. It was the seat of the Dukes of Mazovia, and then – in the 15th century

Warsaw. Krakowskie Przedmieście Street forms part of the old Royal Route leading from the Royal Castle, via Łazienki Park, to the Palace in Wilanów.

Warsaw's Castle Square, with the Column of King Zygmunt III Waza in the foreground.

Warsaw. The Old Town Market Square with the Mermaid Statue.

Warsaw. A portrait of King Stanisław August Poniatowski by Marcello Bacciarelli in the Royal Castle's Marble Room.

Warsaw. The Łazienki Park and Palace complex with its neo-Classical Palace on the Island. This was the seat of Poland's last King, Stanisław August Poniatowski, who reigned until 1795.

– the place at which the Polish-Lithuanian parliaments were convened and the Kings elected. Nevertheless, it only became a royal place of residence – and hence the capital of Poland – in the late 16th and early 17th centuries. As the years passed, Warsaw flourished at times, then crashed at others. The Swedish invasion, the Partitions and of course especially the two World Wars were terribly hard on the city. Indeed, the Nazis reduced left-bank Warsaw to rubble – almost literally. Thus, just about everything one sees in today's Warsaw centre (including the parts that appear to be centuries old) were rebuilt in the late 1940s onward. Thus, Warsaw's must-see Old Town is not old at all, but is nevertheless

Warsaw. Wilanów, one of Poland's finest palatial residences, built for the summer use of King Jan III Sobieski. Here the front elevation of the 17th-century palace.

Warsaw. In the city centre, the skyscrapers of today rub shoulders
with the Socialist-Realist Palace of Culture and Science completed
in 1955. The characteristic building on the left is Złota 44, known
popularly as "The Sail", and designed by Daniel Libeskind.

Warsaw. The Polin Museum of the History of Polish Jews
opened its doors in 2013. It finds itself in a place that was
once the heart of Warsaw's Jewish district, and later
of the Nazis' notorious Warsaw Ghetto.

a World Heritage Site as an example of faithful
reconstruction from its pre-War state, in many
cases down to the finest detail, and with the
surviving original fragments reincorporated into
the structure. The Royal Castle is in a similar
situation, looking exactly as it did centuries ago,
but having been started in the 1970s.

The Wilanów Park and Palace is another
attractive complex to visit, this time on the
outskirts of Warsaw at the end of the so-called
Royal Route that passes all the way from the Old
Town, and takes in the exquisite Łazienki Park,
with its several (also mainly rebuilt) palaces en
route. All told, the Trakt Królewski as it is known
takes in the Krakowskie Przedmieście, Nowy

Warsaw. The Copernicus (Kopernik) Science Centre is one
of Warsaw's newer places to visit, only opened in 2010.
It draws in thousands every day.

Świat and Aleje Ujazdowskie thoroughfares, all attractive and worth a stroll, with their many churches, palaces and stylish tenement houses. A quite different scene is that of the city centre proper, dominated as it is by the imposingly stark Socialist-Realist architecture of the Palace of Culture and Science. The right-bank part of Warsaw (known as Praga) preserves a more-significant amount of pre-War architecture, while some of the older factories have even been made over into centres of culture and entertainment. An example of the Mazovian Gothic style is provided by the impressive ruins of the castle

Jadwisin. This village along the Narew was the place selected by the Radziwiłłs in the late 19th century, as they commenced with the building of a palatial residence paying homage to the architecture of the French Renaissance.

The Zegrze Reservoir, formed by the damming of the Narew, is a place for Varsovians to unwind at weekends.

Sierpc. The Outdoor Museum features the folk architecture of northern Mazowsze. Each Palm Sunday, outdoor events are held here, in association with the traditions of this major church holiday.

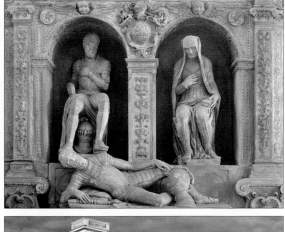

Płock, one of Mazowsze's oldest settlements, dates back
to the 8th century. Its Neo-Classical Town Hall from
the early 19th century has an octagonal tower.

Drobin is a small Mazowsze-region town with a real treasure
in the form of the Renaissance-style tomb of the Kryski family
in the parish church. The artist behind this was most likely
the renowned Santi Gucci.

Sanniki, A neo-Renaissance palace stylised as an Italian villa.
A statue of Fryderyk Chopin stands in front of it.

Żelazowa Wola. The Neo-Classical manor
house is the Fryderyk Chopin Museum.

Czerwińsk was once a centre of trade along the Vistula.
It features a monastery of canons-regular
with a Romanesque church.

Ciechanów – the Castle of the Dukes of Masovia, which was built to a square plan in 1429, albeit with cylindrical towers at each corner for added strength.

Pułtusk on the Narew, former seat of the Bishops of Płock. The Town Hall in the market square with the 16thc. tower and the Bishops' Palace, now Polonia House, in the background.

Zuzela, the brithpalce of cardinal Stefan Wyszyński, Primate of Poland till 1981. A classroom in the former school.

Łyse is a centre of Kurpie-region folk culture known for its "longest palm" contest on Palm Sunday.

Liw. The remains of the castle of the Dukes of Mazovia, where the keep and 18th century manor hold the Museum of Arms and Armour.

in Czersk, as well as the brick-built fortress of the Dukes of Mazovia in Ciechanów. The most beautifully-sited town is Pułtusk, whose centre is on an island created by the River Narew. Here we find one of the longest market squares in Europe, the castle of the Bishops of Płock and the Gothic-Renaissance collegiate church. In Żelazowa Wola, birthplace of Fryderyk Chopin, the country manor house holds a museum devoted to the great composer, and summer concerts of his music are often organised. The manor in Czarnolas is in turn the place of birth and residence of Jan Kochanowski, a poet of the Renaissance whose life and works are celebrated in the museum established here. But Mazowsze is not only cities and museums,

Węgrów was a privately-owned town for much of its history. The Baroque-style Church of the Assumption features design work by Tilmann van Gameren.

Siedlce is one of the largest cities in today's Mazowieckie Voivodeship. The old Town Hall from the mid-18th century now serves museum functions.

Andrzejewo. An interesting coffered ceiling in the Gothic-style church.

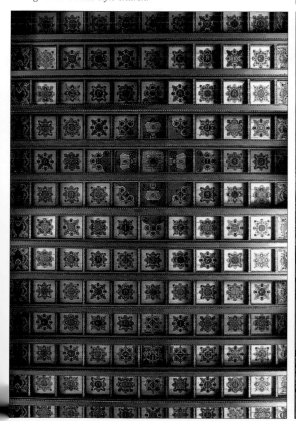

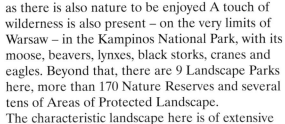

In Żyrardów, the 19th-century factory estate engineered by Frenchman Filip de Girard. This is the view from the parish church of the restored cotton-mill building.

Czersk. The ruins of the 14th-15th century castle, as destroyed by the Swedes, and then the Siedmiogród army.

Sulejówek is a town just outside Warsaw that features the Milusin Villa. Now a museum, this was the home of Józef Piłsudski in the 1920s. The Monument to the Marshal was unveiled in 2010.

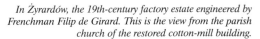

as there is also nature to be enjoyed A touch of wilderness is also present – on the very limits of Warsaw – in the Kampinos National Park, with its moose, beavers, lynxes, black storks, cranes and eagles. Beyond that, there are 9 Landscape Parks here, more than 170 Nature Reserves and several tens of Areas of Protected Landscape.

The characteristic landscape here is of extensive plains with rows of pollarded willows along roads and tracks.

Though this region does not have a great abundance of bodies of water, an area not far from the capital is the Zegrze Reservoir, where rest and recreation can be had in the many holiday centres, and a sail or trip by passenger ferry enjoyed.

Radziejowice. The Neo-Gothic castle is linked via a gallery with the Baroque/Neo-Classical palace.

Czarnolas. The Jan Kochanowski Musem in a 19th-century manor-house designed by Jakub Kubicki.

Radom is a large Mazowsze town that was once, however, across the border in Małopolska. The old Town Hall from the 19th century was constructed to a Henryk Marconi design.

Chlewiska: its 19th-century steelworks complex is today the Museum of Technology.

Szydłowiec. The Gothic-style Parish Church of St. Sigismund from the 15th century.

Iłża. The panorama of the city perpetuating medieval architectural plans. Viewed from the bishop's castle.

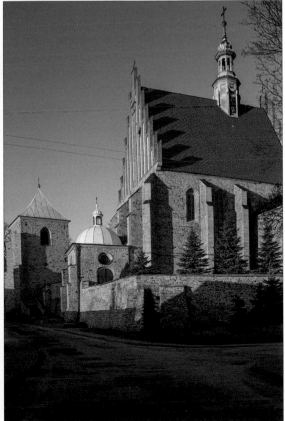

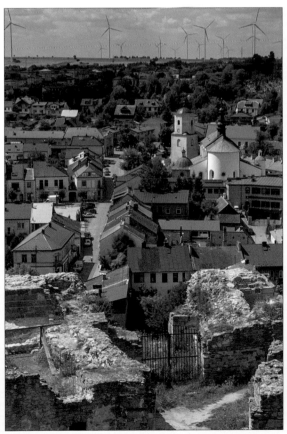

7 ŁÓDZKIE
VOIVODESHIP (ŁÓDŹ)

Capital: ŁÓDŹ

Łódź voivodeship is in central Poland, comprising part of historical Mazovia plus the Sieradz and Łęczyca areas. The history of most of the area resembles that of Mazovia. The capital and main industrial district is the city of Łódź, which obtained its town rights in the 15th century, but was in the hands of the Bishopric of Włocławek until 1798. The first cotton mills and weaving mills appeared there at the beginning of the 19th century. It was not long before the liberal customs regulations regarding trade with Russia – and the unlimited export of textiles to that country this allowed – provoked major growth in the textile industry. This was to ensure that the city had the world's biggest textile factories by the end of the 19th century. Łódź became a cosmopolitan city, with only half of the 600,000-strong population in the inter-War period being Polish (the remainder largely Jewish and German). Immediately after the War, only 250,000 inhabitants were left.

Most of the heritage architecture in Łódź dates back to the 19th century. Particularly characteristic features here are the factory complexes (the owner's mansion plus factory and residential blocks for workers). There are

Łódź. Izrael Poznański's Mansion was designed by Adolf Zeligson and constructed in 1902. The Dining Room offers its most imposing interior.

Łódź. The Ogrodowa Street entrance gate with part of the 1872-1892 mill complex belonging to Izrael Poznański (just near his Mansion).

The Scheilbler Mansion in Łódź. This Neo-Classical/Neo-Renaissance palace has not only stylish rooms, but also a Museum of Cinematography.

also quite a few tenement houses in the Secessionist and Eclectic styles, especially along Piotrkowska Street, regarded as one of Europe's longest commercial thoroughfares. The old factory of Ludwig Geyer today houses the Museum of the Textile Industry, with its very rich and interesting collections, while the reconstructed Herbst Mansion is a museum of 19th century interiors from the big houses of the Łódź industrialists. A good example of a successful marriage between preserved 19th-century architecture and contemporary is the weaving-mill complex, together with the magnificent mansion of magnate Izrael Poznański. The latter's mill

Łódź. Piotrkowska Street. The illumination here picks out the decorative features of facades in the context of a Festival of Light organised annually since 2011.

Nieborów Palace, containing the painting gallery and ancient sculpture collection founded in the 18th century.

Arkadia, the romantic landscape park.

Łowicz is a town on the River Bzura which features the Basilica of the Assumption, including this Renaissance-style tomb of Marcin Śleszyński and his wife Anna.

Boguszyce. The village includes the 16th-century Church of St. Stanisław, with its well-preserved Renaissance polychromy.

Maurzyce, and the Łowicz Ethnographic Park. Here the interior of a country cottage from the late 19th and early 20th centuries.

has become the Manufaktura shopping and entertainment complex, while the mansion once called Łódź's answer to the Louvre houses the Museum of the City of Łódź. Łódź is also the city of Polish cinematography, with the film and theatre school being located here, as well as high-quality film studios. Film festivals are also held here, and even celebrity film premieres. It was in the interestingly outfitted Scheibler Palace that scenes from Andrzej Wajda's epic "The Promised Land" were filmed. The Museum of Cinematography is housed here today. One of the voivodeship's more

Oporów. Chivalrous interiors of the oft-rebuilt castle now house museum exhibits.

*Łowicz. The colourful Corpus Christi
procession with its folk costumes.*

*Łęczyca. Remaining from the 14th-century castle is the western
wing with the "New House" housing the castle museum.*

beautiful attractions is Arkadia – a Romantic-
style landscaped park laid out in the 18th
century. It boasts a lake with two islands and
interesting vegetation, as well as Neo-Gothic
and Neo-Classical park buildings scattered
around it. The Park was laid out by the
landowner in nearby Nieborów, where a fine
Baroque palace of beautiful interiors set in
parkland boasts a wealth of artwork. Other
palaces are to be visited in Walewice,
Poddębice, Białaczów, Wolbórz (the Palaces
of the Bishops of Kujawy), Pabianice and
Skierniewice. The region's several castles
include those: of the Dukes of Mazovia in
Rawa Mazowiecka, of the Archbishops of
Gniezno in Uniejów and of King Kazimierz

*Tum near Łęczyca and the 12th-century Romanesque-style
Collegiate Church of the Assumption and Saint Aleksy.*

Walewice has a Neo-Classical palace associated with Maria Walewska, famed for her romance with Napoleon.

Spycimierz not far from Uniejów. On Corpus Christi day, the processional route is strewn with flowers creating a colourful carpet.

Poddębice. The southern elevation of the Renaissance-style country house dating back to 1610 consists of a cloister topped off with a triangular apex.

Sieradz. Members of the Sieradzanie folk ensemble sport their regional dress.

the Great in Łęczyca. There is also a 14th-century Gothic castle in Oporów, as well as impressive ruins of a Gothic-Renaissance castle at Drzewica. In turn, among the many old churches, the most noteworthy are the Romanesque collegiate church in Tum, as well as the priceless wooden church in Boguszyce, the monastery and church in Paradyż, the fortified Cistercian monastery complex in Sulejów, and the churches in Gidle, Łask and Inowłódz. Łódź voivodeship also includes the Łowicz and Opoczno area, renowned for its rich folk

Uniejów. The remodelled castle dating back to the 14th century was once the residence of Bishops.

Wielgomłyny – the Baroque interiors of St. Stanisław's Church in what was once a Paulite monastery complex.

Popowice. A 16th c. wooden church with shingle roof.

In Ożarów, a single-storey timber-built manor house from 1757 is the seat of the Museum of Manorial Interiors.

Sulejów – one of the best-preserved fortified Cistercian monasteries in Europe.

Inowłódz. The Romanesque Church of St. Giles from 1086 – as reconstructed in the years 1936-1938.

traditions, including in apparel. The ladies' folk costume here is considered one of Poland's most beautiful. Lipce Reymontowskie in turn has a museum to Władysław Reymont, with a biographical exhibition devoted to the Nobel-prizewinning writer, as well as ethnographic collections. Finally, a fine dendrological park and alpinarium can be enjoyed at Rogów.

Opoczno is a town located on the old frontier between Mazowsze (the former Masovia) and Małopolska ("Little Poland"). Here, the 19th-century Renaissance-style castle (which stands in the place of a still-earlier one).

Wolbórz was a seat of the Bishops of Kujavia in the whole period from the 13th to the 18th centuries. The Baroque-era version of their Palace was designed by Franciszek Placidi.

8 WIELKOPOLSKIE
VOIVODESHIP (GREATER POLAND)

Capital: **POZNAŃ**

Poland's second largest voivodeship, it takes in most of historical Wielkopolska (Greater Poland), which is considered the cradle of the country's statehood. It was from here that the first dynasty of Polish rulers, the Piast family, came. Among their number was Duke Mieszko I, who based himself in Gniezno, and thus gave Poland its first capital. Today the townscape there is dominated by the Cathedral Basilica containing one of Europe's finest examples of Romanesque art in the form of the 12th century bronze doors. Relics of St. Adalbert are also to be seen here in a silver casket, along with a Gothic-style crucifix from the 15th century and other valuable works of art. When the Kings of Poland decamped to the new capital, Kraków, Gniezno declined in significance, leaving Poznań to take on the role of Wielkopolska's leading city. It had also once been a city of Kings, being a defensive settlement from the 9th century on, as well as the country's first Bishopric from 968 A.D. The oldest part in existence to day is on Ostrów Tumski island, where the 14th century Cathedral of Sts. Peter and Paul stands in the place of the aforementioned 9th century fortifications. The remains of Poland's first rulers, Mieszko I

Poznań. The Old Market Square with its interestingly arcaded Town Hall.

Poznań. Standing in the oldest part of the town is the monumental Cathedral of Sts. Peter and Paul.

*Rogalin. This small village on the Warta boasts a Rococo/
Neo-Classical style palace in whose design both Domenico Merlini
and Jan Christian Kamsetzer had a hand.*

*Kórnik. The original castle was extensively remodelled
in the English neo-Gothic style in the 19th century.*

and Bolesław Chrobry ("the Brave") lie here.
The many other fine old buildings include
those of the Old Town – dating from the mid
13th century, the castle on Przemysław's Hill,
the Neo-Classical Raczyński Library (whose
faćade is modelled on that of the Louvre)
and a host of churches and palaces.
The regular Market Square includes the
Renaissance Town Hall with characteristic
arcaded façade and ornate billy-goats which
battle daily on the stroke of 12 midday.
Poznań is a famed commercial centre, with its
famous Fairs marking a tradition established
in the Middle Ages. The first modern fairs
were the national events from 1921 and the

*Koszuty. A late 18th century manor house,
now housing the regional museum.*

Gniezno. Cathedral, the unique Romanesque Gniezno Doors from the 12th century depict scenes from the life of St. Adalbert.

Ostrów Lednicki – ruins of an early-Romanesque palatium dating from the 10th century.

Czerniejewo. The conference room in the Baroque/Neo-Classical palace, which was restored after wartime devastation.

Ląd. The Gothic ambulatory in the former Cistercian monastery complex.

Ciążeń. The Rococo palace of the Bishops of Poznań. It holds the Poznań University Library with its collections of masonic literature.

International Fairs from 1925. It needs to be recalled that this was not always a Polish centre. The Partitions left the city in Prussian hands, and the new masters' restrictive regulations and high taxes for Polish landowners were designed to ensure the speediest possible takeover of their assets by Germanic newcomers. In opposition to this, the keeping of land in Polish hands became a patriotic duty – and one that could only be achieved through outstanding management based on mechanisation and the latest cultivation techniques. It is probably for this

Miłosław. The 19th-century palace modeled on Italian villas and surrounded by a park.

Pyzdry. Fragments of 14th-18th century frescoes in the cloisters of a former Franciscan monastery.

Biechowo, whose Late Baroque monastery complex with its 15th-century Pieta makes this a place of piligrimage.

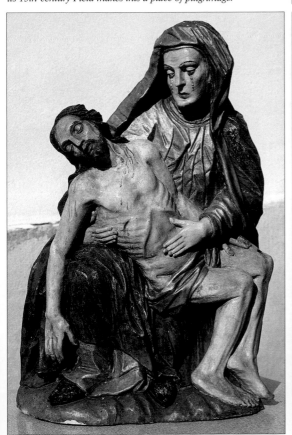

61

Koło. The ruins of the Mediaeval castle located on heights overlooking the Warta.

The Sanctuary at Licheń. This is the Catholic place of worship in Poland enclosing the greatest volume of space. It was built with money donated in the second half of the 20th century and is a tangible tribute to the activeness of the Church in this country during the era of Polish Pope John Paul II.

reason that the farming in Wielkopolska was later to earn its reputation as Poland's most advanced. Wielkopolska voivodeship has a particularly noteworthy collection of old magnates' residences. A beautiful palace and park complex in Kórnik, for example, was last owned by Władysław Zamoyski, who gave it over to the nation in 1924. Today it houses a museum of interiors, with rich collections of furniture, paintings, sculptures and porcelain, as well as a library. Rogalin boasts a Rococo/Neo-Classical palace in parkland that

Lubstówek. St Matthew's church. A wooden construction from 1639.

Made attractive by the presence of lakes, the area around Konin is a place of rest and relaxation for the inhabitants of the town itself.

Opatówek. Once a 19th century cloth manufacture, now a Museum of Industrial History.

Russów. At the ethnographical exhibition in the manor park – the interior of a peasants' hut.

Śmiełów. The late 18th century palace with its Neo-Classical column portico.

includes oaks of girths in the range 7-9 m. The former coach-house has a collection of old coaches and carriages. Rydzyna is famous for its beautiful castle, while the park in Śmiełów rewards the visitor to the Neo-Classical palace complex with its museum devoted to Adam Mickiewicz. Memorabilia connected with the poet is gathered here, as are collections of European painting. In turn, an exceptionally original, Greek cross-shaped wooden hunting lodge can be seen in Antonin. Other interesting palaces and manors are to be found in Pawłowice, Czerniejewo, Dobrzyca, Koszuty, Manieszki, Turew and Miłosław. Surviving in Gołuchów

Sulmierzyce is a town on the Leszczyńska Plateau. The arcaded wooden town hall from 1743 houses the Regional Museum.

Kalisz is probably the oldest town in Poland. Here, the contemporary Church of Divine Mercy.

is a castle that now presents collections of oriental and antique art. Further castles are to be found in Koźmin Wielkopolski and in Szamotuły. Also of great historical value and beauty are some of the examples of religious architecture, like the monastery complex in Ląd, the sanctuary to the Virgin Mary in Gostyń, the monasteries or convents in Koło, Kazimierz Biskupi and Pyzdry, and the churches in Kościan, Kościelec and Piła. An exceptional place attracting pilgrims from throughout the country has been the sanctuary at Licheń Stary. The goal is

Bralin. The 1711 "Na Pólku" church of indulgence is one of the most original wooden churches in Wielkopolska.

Gołuchów. Zamek z XVI wieku, przebudowany w stylu renesansu francuskiego w XIX wieku, usytuowany w malowniczym parku angielskim.

Antonin. The wooden hunters' lodge from the early 19th century. Palace interior: three-storey hall with ceiling supported by one column-chimney.

Wolsztyn. Steam engine Ok-1 in Europe's last working engine house.

Gostyń-Głogówko, with its Philippinian monastery complex, Sanctuary to the Virgin Mary and 17th-century church.

Lubiń. A Rococo stall with statuettes of angels carrying musical instruments, in the Benedictine church presbytery.

the painting of the Licheń Mother of God formerly placed above the high altar in the Neo-Gothic church, but now in the basilica (Poland's largest). Wielkopolskie voivodeship also boasts superb nature and landscapes, with the Lakeland, 12 Landscape Parks and around 100 Nature Reserves. Also within the voivodeship, and not far from the city of Poznań, is the Wielkopolski National Park.

Rydzyna. Rich stuccos in the Marine's Room of the Baroque castle.

Sieraków. 17th century former Bernardine church in the Late-Renaissance style.

Wieleń. The two-winged Baroque palace of the Sapieha family from the mid-18th century.

Międzychód, a holiday resort for Poznań inhabitants. Market square houses.

9 LUBUSKIE
VOIVODESHIP (LUBUSZ)

Capital: **GORZÓW WIELKOPOLSKI**

This is one of Poland's smaller voivodeships, covering less than 14,000 km². In the west it borders with Germany across the Nysa Łużycka and Oder Rivers. It takes in the eastern part of the Lubusz Land from history, with the remaining part – including the town of Lubusz itself – being German territory. Most of the present inhabitants of the Polish part are descendents of settlers brought in after 1945, since these lands were not Polish before the War. They came, in turn, from lands that were in pre-War Poland, but were ceded to the Soviet Union when hostilities ceased. The authorities sit in two centres, i.e. Gorzów Wielkopolski as the seat of the provincial governor and Zielona Góra as the location of the elected regional assembly. Gorzów was founded in the mid 13th century, surrounded by strong fortifications and thus able to grow to become an important settlement in the Neumark region. A further flowering of the city came in the 18th century, as trade was enlivened by the completion of the Bydgoszcz Canal. This connected the Vistula and Oder basins. The oldest monument in Gorzów is its Gothic cathedral, while remnants of the defensive walls and granaries from the late 18th century are still to be found. Zielona Góra

Gorzów Wielkopolski is (another) town spread picturesquely across seven hills.

Gorzów Wielkopolski. The oldest place of worship here is the Cathedral of the Assumption, which is Gothic in style and boasts a massive tower on its west side.

Zielona Góra. The Old Market Square with its 17th-century Town Hall and view of the Mother of God of Częstochowa Church.

won its town rights in 1323, at which time it lay within the Dukedom of Głogów. At the beginning of the 16th century it was in turn part of the Czech lands for a couple of decades, before passing on to the Habsburgs. It became Prussian in 1742, and only came to Poland after the Second World War. The older parts include fine churches, parts of the city walls, and the Town Hall on the Old Market Square. Zielona Góra and its surroundings were once famous for the production of wine. Two hundred years ago, there were more than 2000 sites here growing vines. By the end of the 20th century, winemaking had almost entirely disappeared from here, but new vineyards have been appearing, and there seems to be a chance for a wine industry in this region to redevelop.

Wschowa is a historic town with Baroque architecture. From this corner we catch a glimpse of the Gothic-Renaissance Town Hall.

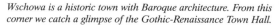

Almost 50% of the voivodeship's area is taken by forests. The largest blocks are the Drawska, Gorzowska, Notecka and Lubuska Forests, as well as the Dolnośląskie and Zielonogórskie Pine Forests. The greater part of the Drawieński National Park is within the limits of the region, which also boasts the Ujście Warty National Park at the confluence point between the Warta and Oder; as well as Landscape Parks and reserves. A large number of Monuments of Nature include the huge oaks in Piotrowice (with girths of 990 cm) and Łęknica (870 cm). Very specific is the transboundary Mużakowski Park, which has been a World Heritage Site in Poland and

Świebodzin. The scene in this small town is dominated by a 33-metre figure of Christ, wearing a 3-metre crown. The whole thing receives a further boost by being located on a mound 16 metres high.

Gościkowo. The former Cistercian church with a two-tower Baroque façade dates back to the 13th century.

Międzyrzecz Fortified Region. A belt of anti-tank obstacles, called "dragon's teeth".

Drezdenko. Buildings of the Old Market Square
with the 19th century court-house.

Rokitno, a centre of the cult of the Virgin Mary,
where the painting in the altar shows
Our Lady of Rokitno.

Pszczew. An 18th century cobbler's house,
now a regional museum.

Strzelce Krajeńskie. The 15th-century Mill Gate guards
the embankment separating the two lakes in the town.

Międzyrzecz. In the Middle Ages, this was the fortified town
defending Wielkopolska against incursions from the west.
Here the remains of King Kazimierz the Great's castle.

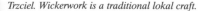
Trzciel. Wickerwork is a traditional lokal craft.

Germany since 2004. Świerkocin has zoo with a safari motif, while the many lakes all have holiday centres. The most popular of all are Lubniewice and Łagów. Many elements of the area's heritage are preserved. Żagan has one of Poland's finest Baroque palaces, as well as a formerly Augustine monastery complex. An interesting park plus palace is to be found in Żary, and there are castles in: Łagów, Sulechów, Kożuchów, Kostrzyn and Międzyrzecz, as well as small fortresses in Lubniewice and Lubsko. Krosno Odrzańskie preserves fragments of a castle of the Piasts, while Sulechów boasts not only a castle, but also stretches of the old ramparts, and a fine old town hall and church. Międzyrzecz also has

Łagów. This 35m tower is part of a castle that belonged to the Order of St. John between the mid-14th and early 19th centuries.

Lubsko. This town's oldest church is that of the Visitation. Some parts of the old walls date back to the late 13th century.

Łęknica – here the Polish part of the Mużakowski Park, which straddles the River Nysa Łużycka, and hence the border with Germany. The viaduct is the former entrance to the Park on the eastern side.

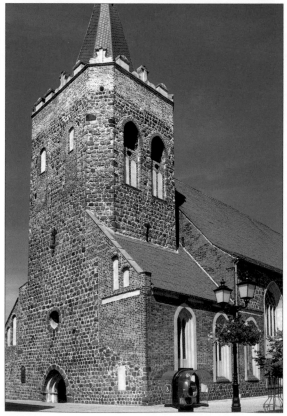

Żagań is a heritage-rich town that features a former Augustinian monastery complex. The Baroque-style Library has original shelving and frescoes by Georg Wilhelm Neunhertz, which date back to 1736.

Buczyny – The Outdoor Museum of the Lusatian Region only commenced with its activity in 1992.

a Neo-Classical town hall and Gothic church. Among the many surviving palaces those worthy of note include the ones in Sława and Kargowa as well as the one hidden among woodland in Rogi. Szprotawa has a church going back to the 18th century, as well as a town hall from a century later. Lovers of military architecture will in turn find the defences of the Międzyrzecz Fortified District of interest. These were erected by the Germans prior to World War II and are the largest of their kind in today's Poland. The underground passages are now home to one of Europe's largest colonies of bats.

Żary is a town in Lusatia which first gained its rights in 1260. Since 2010, its Market Square has boasted Telemann's Bench – a testament to the composer' time spent here at the beginning of the 18th century.

10 DOLNOŚLĄSKIE
VOIVODESHIP (LOWER SILESIA)

Capital: **WROCŁAW**

This voivodeship is in the south west of Poland, where it borders onto the Czech Republic and Germany. The relief is rather varied, including plains in the north and the Sudety mountain chain in the south. The central part includes the Ślęża massif, from which the Polish name for Silesia, Śląsk, most probably derives. This was a cult centre in pre-Christian times, though all that can be seen of this now are some stone walls and carvings. The voivodeship capital, Wrocław, is one of Poland's oldest cities. In the year 1000, a bishopric subordinated to the Archbishopric of Gniezno was founded here. In turn, it was at the beginning of the

13th century that town rights were obtained. The destruction by the Tartars in 1241 and various changes of allegiance, notwithstanding, Wrocław never stopped developing. Only in the course of the Thirty Years' War and Silesian Wars was there any let-up in the growth. Wrocław became Prussian from 1763 and – as still a German city in World War II – was subject to heavy Allied bombing. Yet today's Wrocław is again a University city full of life and interesting historical buildings like the 14th-15th century Gothic Town Hall, the famous Leopoldin Hall at the University in the former Jesuit college, the 13th-15th century Gothic Cathedral of St. John and

The Old Town Market Square in Wrocław has this characteristic, richly-decorated Gothic Town Hall.

Wrocław, a settlement of the Slavic tribe known as the Ślężanie in the first millennium. Ostrów Tumski, St. John the Baptist's Cathedral..

The Baroque Leopoldin Lecture Hall built in 1732 to the design by Franz Joseph Mangoldt and Johann Christoph Handke, as part of a complex of buildings that made up Wrocław University.

Wrocław. The Panorama of the Battle of Racławice is the work of a team of painters led by Tadeusz Styka and Wojciech Kossak. Dating back to 1894, it portrays Tadeusz Kościuszko's victory against the Russians a century earlier.

many other churches, monasteries and convents, tenement houses and palaces. The Centennial Hall is a further noteworthy building, erected in the years 1911-1913 and UNESCO World Heritage-listed since 2006. A particular attraction is the Battle of Racławice Panorama, a painting by Jan Styka and Wojciech Kossak which was produced in 1894 – the hundredth anniversary of this first engagement in the Kościuszko Insurrection. As a city on the River Oder, Wrocław has over 100 bridges over the main river and its

Wrocław's Centennial Hall is a reinforced-concrete construction dating back to 1911-13, and to a Max Berg design.

The Gate of Legnica Castle, which was the seat of the Piasts of Legnica-Brzeg, the last line of the first Polish dynasty.

Oława. In the 13th century, the building of a castle here coincided with the granting of town rights. The castle was remodelled in the Renaissance era (16th century), and then made over once again 100 years later – this time into the Baroque style.

Oleśnica. The courtyard in the Castle of the Dukes of Oleśnica, which was built of brick and stone and has a cylindrical corner tower.

The Milicz Ponds – established in the late 13th and early 14th centuries for the breeding of fish, they are now a protected refuge for birds.

Lubin is a town known for producing copper and silver. The castle chapel (now an art gallery) is a leftover from the Mediaeval castle with parts of its defensive walls.

Trzebnica. The Church of Sts. Bartholomew and Jadwiga. The sarcophagus of St. Jadwiga of Silesia was made from black and pink marbles in the years 1679-1680, along with the saint's likeness from white alabaster.

Lubiąż. The Prince's Hall with its Franz Joseph Mangoldt sculpturework is within the Abbot's Palace – just one element to the Baroque-style Cistercian monastery complex.

Karkonosze. The Sudety Mountains are much visited by tourists drawn to their beautiful and unique landscape.

numerous branches. The best-known bridge of all is the Grunwaldzki suspension bridge. The city also boasts Poland's largest and most famous zoo, which was founded in 1865. Other large centres in the voivodeship are Legnica, Wałbrzych and Jelenia Góra. In the place where Legnica now stands there was a Slavic defensive settlement as early as in the 8th century. Later on this was the capital of the Piast Dukedom of Legnica. The city has Silesia's finest Baroque place of worship – the church of John the Baptist, as well as the castle of the Dukes of Legnica,

Świeradów-Zdrój has been renowned as a spa since the mid-16th century. This promenade hall dates back to1899. however.

In Leśna, the Gothic/Renaissance-style Czocha Castle has a characteristic 14th-century cylindrical tower.

Płakowice. Featuring Renaissance-era decoration, this beautiful gate leads through to the arcaded courtyard of the 16th-century castle.

Cieplice Śląskie-Zdrój. One of the oldest Lower Silesian health resorts, it has formally been a district of Jelenia Góra since 1976.

Grodziec has a castle close by the village of the same name. This is a Gothic/Renaissance high castle, with a moat and gated entrance.

Strzegom. The interior of the Gothic-style Church of Sts. Peter and Paul has bas-relief stonework with epitaph plates among other things.

the Market Square with its Baroque Town Hall from the 18th century and tenement houses form the 16th. Wałbrzych was a place of industry from almost the start of its existence: iron ore was worked here as early as in the 14th century, coal from the 16th century on. Various heritage buildings remain, and some have museums. The now-closed "Julia" Mine houses the Museum of Industry and Technology, for example.

Świdnica. The Augsburg-Evangelical Church was erected in the years 1656-8. Thanks to the galleries, the Baroque interior seems more like that of a theatre than a church.

Karpacz. The 13th century Evangelical Wang Church brought from Norway in the 19th century.

Krzeszów. The polychromy on the ceiling of the Church of the Assumption, which is known as the "Pearl of the Silesian Baroque".

Henryków – the ex-Cistercian Church of the Assumption and St. John the Baptist. The ornate sculpturework of the interior was added during Baroque remodelling in the 17th century.

Książ. The largest castle of the Piasts in Silesia, once a border fort, erected in the 13th century and rebuilt as recently as in the 19th. Here the Ballroom or Maximilian Room.

Zagórze Śląskie. The Grodno Castle was built in the 15th century, only to be remodelled in Renaissance style in the following century. This sgraffito decoration is from that time.

Also within the city limits is the castle of the Hochbergs in Książ, which is the largest in Lower Silesia. Extending around the castle is a landscaped park renowned for its rhododendrons. Jelenia Góra developed thanks to weaving and mining, but it owes its current popularity to tourism. Within its boundaries lies Cieplice Śląskie-Zdrój – a spa famous as early as in the Middle Ages. Other well-known health resorts in Lower Silesia are Kudowa, Lądek, Polanica and Duszniki. Lower Silesia is famous for its many castles. Apart from the aforementioned one in Książ,

Wojanów. Sitting in an extensive landscaped park here is a Renaissance/Neo-Gothic palace with four arquière towers.

Kamieniec Ząbkowicki. The 19th-century Neo-Gothic castle was ruined as recently as in the post-War era.

Czermna near Kudowa-Zdrój. The "Chapel of Skulls" brings together the remains of those who fell in the Silesian Wars or cholera epidemics of the 18th century.

there are better-known examples in places like Głogów, Bolków, Grodziec, Oleśnica, near Leśna (Czocha) and Sobieszów (Chojnik). There are also many old palaces, as at Milicz, Wleń and Warmątowice. Most localities retain some of their old architecture, often in the form of beautiful churches, market squares with town halls and stylish tenement houses, as at Bystrzyca Kłodzka, Gryfów Śląski, Lądek Zdrój, Lwówek Śląski, Oława, Środa Śląska and Świdnica. A 14th-century tower home is a further attraction, situated in Siedlęcin. The many sacred buildings include the monasteries in Henryków, Kłodzko, Krzeszów, Lubiąż and Trzebnica, the Abbey in Kamieniec Ząbkowicki, and two well-

Złoty Stok. There was a goldmine in operation here from the 13th century through to 1962. Today, some of the passages and galleries are open to visitors.

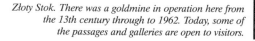

Wambierzyce. The Sanctuary of Our Lady known as the Silesian Jerusalem. Leading up to the Late Baroque Church of the Visitation are some 56 steps.

preserved (World Heritage Site) "Peace Churches" in Jawór and Świdnica, so-called because they were erected following the Thirty Years' War. A unique feature is the 13th-century wooden Wang Chapel in Karpacz, brought here from Norway in 1842. Also noteworthy is the sanctuary in Wambierzyce from the late 17th and early 18th centuries, known as the Silesian Jerusalem with its Stations of the Cross and almost 100 calvary shrines. The greatest tourist hotspots in the region are the Karkonosze Mountains. Many trails make this a paradise for walkers, and the Karkonoski National Park (also a UNESCO Biosphere

Chełmsko Śląskie. An old complex of weavers' houses with both dwellings and places of work.

Błędne Skały – a landscape reserve with a rock labyrinth in the Stołowe Mountains.

Góry Stołowe. Szczeliniec Wielki is the highest peak in the Stołowe Mountains (at 919 m a.s.l.). It was a popular destination for trips as early as in the 18th century.

The Niedźwiedzia (Bear) Cave in the Sudety Mountains below Śnieżnik has Poland's best examples of stalactities and stalagmities.

Kłodzko. The Gothic-style stone bridge has Baroque carvings of saints.

Duszniki-Zdrój. The Baroque-style paper mill now serves as the seat of the Museum of the Paper Industry.

Reserve) is the centre of everything. Another interesting region is the Kłodzko Basin with its many sources of healing waters, as well as the Sowie Mountains – Poland's oldest, being of Pre-Cambrian shalcs. Rather newer are the Second World War tunnels dug into them by the Nazis, some of which can be visited. The Stołowe ("Table") Mountains are also intriguing where the rock forms take on a host of different shapes. There is a National Park here too, as well as the famous Błędne Skały Nature Reserve. This is in fact just one of the voivodeship's ca. 70 Nature Reserves; and there are also 12 Landscape Parks in this region.

Kochanów. A mediaeval chair of judgment made of stone.

11 OPOLSKIE
VOIVODESHIP (OPOLE)

Capital: **OPOLE**

This smallest of Poland's voivodeships covers c. 9500 km². The north and central part is in the Silesian Lowland, with the part north of Opole being termed the Opole Plain. The Opawskie Hills lie in the south. The history of these lands do not differ greatly from those of neighbouring Lower Silesia. Like other Silesian fiefs, the Dukedom of Opole was a Czech district under the Habsburgs, before it passed on to Prussia. A large number of the people living here are still of German origin, hence the lobby for the voivodeship to be created in the first place. They have their own schools, organisations and members of parliament. However ethnic Czechs and Ukrainians also live here. The voivodeship capital is Opole, which was founded at the beginning of the 13th century where an even older defended settlement had stood. The Old Town here is of interest, surrounded by Baroque tenement houses, and there is a Gothic Cathedral, the remains of the ramparts and the Piastowska Tower surveying all of them. Opole is famous for the Song Festival, while a further dose of atmosphere (of "Little Venice") is imparted

Opole. The Gothic-style interiors of the Holy Cross Cathedral, with the view of the central nave and transept, as well as the 18th-century Main Altar.

Opole, with old houses by the Młynówką, one of the branches of the Oder.

Opole. The Old Town's Krakowska Street is now pedestrianised, It starts at the Market Square, though here part of the tower of the Neo-Gothic Town Hall is to be seen. That was modelled on the Palazzo Vecchio in Florence.

Moszna near Opole has an Eclectic-style castle built at the end of the 19th century.

by the picturesque buildings along a branch of the Oder called the Młynówka. The second largest urban area is that of Kędzierzyn-Koźle, which emerged in 1975 with the linking of the four towns of Kędzierzyn, Koźle, Kłodnica and Sławęcice. Another quite large and significant town is Nysa, which remains one of Silesia's most beautiful places, despite the destruction wrought in World War II. The Old Town represents Opole-Silesia's finest built heritage. Like Nysa, many of the region's other towns came through the War with monuments intact. One such place is Brzeg, with its Renaissance castle

Karłowice is a village with a knights' castle dating back to the Middle Ages. In fact it is one of the best-preserved fortifications anywhere in the Opole region.

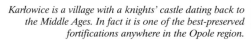

Michalice. The name of this village probably relates to St. Michael – the patron saint of the wooden church here dating back to the early 17th century.

Łosiów. This small village boasts a country seat from the early 20th century, as surrounded by extensive heritage parkland.

Kościerzyce. The Gothic-style Church of the Assumption from the late 14th and early 15th centuries. It forms an item along the "Brest Polychromy Trail" (of 14 rural churches, with several retaining their original painted murals).

nicknamed Silesia's Wawel, the Piast school building from 1564, the most precious Renaissance Town Hall in Silesia and churches. Similar is Głogówek, with its Old Town and Town Hall, churches and ruined castle. Paczków is in turn famous for its Gothic town walls with 19 towers and 4 gates, as well as the Gothic fortified church, with that most necessary of items in a siege, a well

Małujowice. St. James's Church is adorned with Mediaeval murals – the best preserved of any along the "Brest Polychromy Trail".

Namysłów. The neglected courtyard of the old castle with its Late Renaissance well.

Brzeg. The Renaissance castle sometimes called "Silesia's Wawel" has a courtyard gate with a richly-decorated entrance façade.

Brzeg. Silesia's most beautiful Renaissance Town Hall.

inside. Otmuchów retains its Renaissance castle with the so-called horse steps. The city is also known for its annual flower festival. South of Opole is Moszna, with its Eclectic palace and stud farm full of English bloodlines. One of Opole-Silesia's most important monuments is in turn the wonderful example of Gothic polychromy in the interior of Małujowice church. Also of note is the untypical wooden place of worship in Olesno, which was raised to a design based on a five-petalled flower. To the south-east of the region's capital is a famous sanctuary

Otmuchów. One of the items of heritage architecture confirming this town's rank historically is the Bishop's Castle. Its flat steps from the 18th century apparently served their purpose as an ill bishop was carried up and down on a litter.

Paczków. A view of the old Church of St. John the Evangelist with the famous defensive walls around the town.

Nysa. The Late Gothic Church of Sts. James and Agnes. The interior has three aisles of uniform height with cross and star vaulting.

Strzelce Opolskie. The 15th-century stone tower along a section of the town walls is from the early 18th century and is the belltower of St. Lawrence's Church.

Ozimek. The 19th-century iron chain-bridge spanning the River Mała Panew represents an outstanding piece of heritage bridge-building.

Krapkowice is a town by the River Oder. Here the 14th-century tower of the Upper Gate.

of Saint Anne's Mountain. Once the site of a pagan cult, this now has a Baroque monastery with a calvary and 30 shrines. In consequence it has long been the most important place of pilgrimage in Silesia. Nature in Opole voivodeship is also noteworthy, given that 34 Nature Reserves and 4 Landscape Parks have been established here.

Góra św. Anny (St. Anne's Mountain) is an extinct volcano featuring a Sanctuary with relics of St. Anne that are a goal for pilgrimages. The Good Friday commemorations here are particularly renowned.

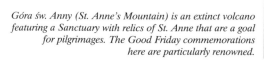

12 ŚLĄSKIE
VOIVODESHIP (SILESIA)

Capital: KATOWICE

This most industrialised of Poland's voivodeships covers 12,300 km² and is inhabited by no fewer than 4.9 million people. This makes it the most densely-populated region in Poland. It borders with the Czech Republic and Slovakia to the south. The heavy industries to have been developed most strongly here are mining (for hard coal), steelmaking, the machinery industry and chemicals. The major aggregation of industry is in the Upper Silesian Industrial District, as well as around Bielsko-Biała, Rybnik and Częstochowa. Katowice is the capital, and at the same time one of Silesia's youngest urban centres (it only obtained town

rights in 1865). It appeared with the dynamic development of industry in the 19th century, and its centre features a Monument to the Silesian Uprisings of 1919, 1920 and 1921. An unusual area worth a visit is the Nikiszowiec quarter of the city – an example of an early working-class housing estate. Other large centres of the Upper Silesian Industrial District are: Chorzów, Sosnowiec, Dąbrowa Górnicza, Bytom, Zabrze, Tychy and Gliwice. In Tarnowskie Góry, the "Black Trout" workings of an 18th-century silver mine can be visited by boating along the flooded tunnels. Zabrze in turn attracts visitors with its museum of the mining industry at the site of the

Katowice. Headquartered in Korfantego Avenue is the Silesian Museum, which was brought into being by a 1929 resolution of the Silesian Assembly.

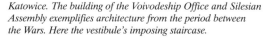

Katowice. The building of the Voivodeship Office and Silesian Assembly exemplifies architecture from the period between the Wars. Here the vestibule's imposing staircase.

Katowice. Built in the years 1908-1915 is the Nikiszowiec workers' estate, including this courtyard between residential buildings.

Queen Luiza mine first worked in 1791 and now of course closed. Chorzów boasts Poland's largest Recreational Park – whose 600 ha include a planetarium, National Stadium, large fairground, centre for water sports, a swimming-pool complex, a chairlift, light railway and zoo, as well as an ethnographic park with an open-air museum devoted to the Upper Silesian countryside. The most beautiful examples of architectural heritage have survived in Będzin (the castle), Cieszyn (the 11th-century Romanesque rotunda, churches, Old Town market square and Town Hall and Gothic style defensive tower), Pszczyna (Old Town, palace

Tarnowskie Góry. A route 1740 m long has been made available to visitors at the Zabytkowa Kopalnia Rud Srebronośnych (Heritage Mine of Silver-Bearing Ores). The Zawałowa Chamber has exhibits that include wooden carts for the transport of mined ore. Listed by UNESCO as World Heritage Sites in 2017.

Toszek. Erected in the 15th century, the Castle of the Dukes of Racibórz and Opole fell into ruin during the 19th century. It was partially rebuilt after World War II.

Będzin – the 14th-century Castle is now a District Museum.

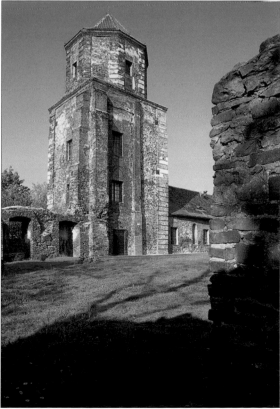

Pietrowice near Raciborz. One of a kind in Poland is this town's "100-Horse Procession" on Easter Monday.

Racibórz is one of the historic seats of the Silesian Princes. Here the Renaissance-style Prison Gate which forms part of the town's ramparts.

Pszczyna. The Neo-Baroque Mansion here was the seat of the Dukes of Hochberg von Pless. It is surrounded by an extensive landscaped park.

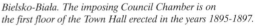

Bielsko-Biała. The imposing Council Chamber is on the first floor of the Town Hall erected in the years 1895-1897.

Cieszyn was first located in 1220. Its Romanesque rotunda church of St. Nicholas dates back to the late 11th and early 12th centuries and is located on Castle Heights.

*The Beskid Śląski range is a densely-forested area
put to intensive tourist use.*

*Cieszyn. A performance by the Janina Marcinkowa
Cieszyn Region Folk Song and Dance Ensemble.*

and outdoor museum), Szczekociny (18th-century Baroque palace), Żywiec (castle with arcaded courtyard) and Bielsko-Biała (15th-century castle, Eclectic-style Town Hall, other Secessionist-style buildings). The voivodeship also includes Poland's most famous sanctuary to the cult of the Virgin Mary with its miraculous likeness of the Mother of God, namely the Jasna Góra Monastery in Częstochowa. Another religious centre of particular significance to Silesians is Piekary Śląskie. Perhaps surprisingly, the voivodeship includes areas of natural beauty also – part of the Kraków-Częstochowa Upland, as well as the Silesian, Żywiec and Small Beskid ranges. The upland supports an interesting tourist path

*Żywiec. The view from the Market Square of the Gothic,
Renaissance and Baroque Church of the Assumption
of Mary. It's stone-built belltower dates back to 1724.*

Mirów. Ruins of the Gothic castle erected in the 14th-century reign of Kazimierz the Great.

Okiennik Wielki is one of the most characteristic of the Jura rocks. Its northern wall stands over ten metres high.

Zawiercie. This well-preserved Jewish Cemetery founded in the early 20th century signifies this town's multicultural past.

Ogrodzieniec. The ruins of the Gothic-Renaissance fort are among Poland s largest (volume 32,000 m³).

The Castle in Bobolice was reconstructed by private owner Jarosław W. Lasecki. Work on it was completed by 2001.

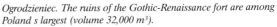

Złoty Potok is a picturesque village featuring the Neo-Classical residence of the Raczyński family. This lion with emblematic cartouche stands by the palace entrance.

known as the "Eagles' Nests" Trail, which links the mediaeval fortresses of Olsztyn, Mirów, Bobolice and Ogrodzieniec, as well as the Jura Fortresses Trail. Olsztyn (near Częstochowa) also has annual outdoor festivals with firework displays and various performances. Popular centres in the aforementioned Beskids include the ski resorts of Szczyrk, Korbielów, Wisła, Ustroń and Brenna. Istebna and Koniaków are in turn villages famed for their folk crafts, e.g. Lacekmaking.

Olsztyn near Częstochowa. The ruins of a 13th-century fortress extend out across the flattish limestone summit here, with the round tower being all that is left of the old upper castle.

Częstochowa. The entrance on to the Jasna Góra Hill from the west side. The destination here – including for pilgrimages from the length and breadth of Poland – is the famous Sanctuary of the Black Madonna.

Częstochowa. The miraculous Madonna of Jasna Góra wears a diamond robe – a unique testament to the jeweller's art.

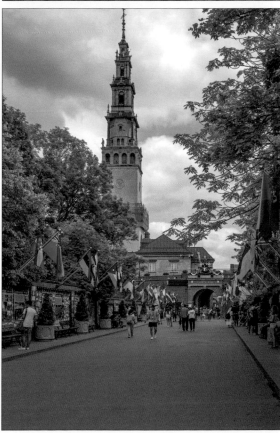

13 ŚWIĘTOKRZYSKIE
VOIVODESHIP

Capital: **KIELCE**

This small voivodeship of 11,700 km² supports c. 1.3 million inhabitants. A region lying between the Rivers Vistula and Pilica and known as the land of Kielce, it was the northern part of the historical Małopolska and was always of great significance in Polish history. The Slav tribe known as the Vistulanians had their state here as early as in the 9th century, becoming Christians by the year 880, or some 86 years before the baptism of Poland's Mieszko I. The Vistulanians came within the state established by Mieszko in the year 990. The Kielce area has an ancient industrial tradition. In the Neolithic period, Krzemionki near Ostrowiec Świętokrzyski had quarries for flint used in the making of tools. In turn, in the first millennium A.D. there was Europe's largest centre producing iron here (with some 300,000 ovens known as dymarki having been found). In Nowa Słupia, the Świętokrzyskie Dymarki celebration represents an annual event attractive to tourists. Copper, silver and lead used in the manufacture of coins were worked here in the Middle Ages, and later also marbles and sandstones fashioned by the area's famous stoneworks. This was also an area of 19th-century metallurgy. To this day,

Kielce. The Bishop's Apartments in the Palace of the Bishops of Kraków feature this plafond from 1683 depicting "The Judgment over the Arians".

Kielce. The front elevation of the Palace of the Bishops of Kraków, which was built between 1637 and 1641. The residential layout here remains very well preserved.

Kielce is a small city in the Świętokrzyskie Mountains. Its Town Square features (has its entire west side taken up by) the Neo-Classical Town Office building.

marbles, limestones, gypsums, sandstones, white clays, ores and glassmaking sands are worked in the area. It is also from the Kielce area that many types of semi-precious stones used in jewellery are obtained. Overall, the area is known as the Staropolskie Industrial District. Unsurprisingly, the dynamic development of industry here in the 19th century encouraged the establishment of Poland's first technical school, the Szkoła Akademiczno-Górnicza (Academic Mining School). Kielce, a city in the hands of the Bishops of Kraków between the 11th and late 18th centuries, is the capital and main industrial settlement of Świętokrzyskie

Tokarnia. The interior of a hut equipped in the original way is to be seen in the Outdoor Museum of the Kielce Countryside.

Chęciny. On the castle mound are the ruins of the fortress where Władysław the Short had his exchequer. It fell into this state in the wake of destruction wrought by the Swedes.

Jaskinia Raj – one of Poland's most beautiful caves, it has a wealth of stalactites and stalagmites.

The Skałki Piekło pod Niekłaniem Nature Reserve. The greatest attractions here take the form of sandstone rocks and pinnacles 2-8 m in height, entirely surrounded by forest.

The Świnia Góra Nature Reserve in turn protects the mixed/brodleaved forest so typical for the Świętokrzyskie Mountains.

Święty Krzyż. East of Kielce, in the Łysa Góra Massif, is a Benedictine Abbey funded by King Bolesław Wrymouth in the 12th century.

voivodeship. Standing in memory of the former owners there is the lovely Bishop's Palace, considered the most beautiful piece of architectural heritage in the city. A second, similarly valuable building is the Baroque Cathedral, with still-surviving elements of the older Romanesque place of worship that came before it. Other large towns or cities in the region are: Ostrowiec Świętokrzyski, Sandomierz, Starachowice and Skarżysko Kamienna. The oldest place on this list is Sandomierz, a walled township as early as in the 10th century and one of Poland's most

Wąchock. The Cistercian Monastery funded in 1179 to this day retains some of its original structures, not least this Refectory building with its ornate Romanesque stonework.

important centres just a century later. Standing as testimony to this history to the present day is the Market Square with Renaissance Town Hall and tenement houses, the Gothic cathedral rebuilt in the Baroque period, the Dominican priory and much else. Other parts preserve history equally well, as sacred architecture (e.g. the Wąchock Romanesque-Gothic Cistercian Abbey complex; the Święty Krzyż Benedictine Monastery erected on the site of an old pagan sanctuary; and Święta Katarzyna) and as temporal buildings (like the palace in Kurozwęki, town walls in Szydłów, and open-air museum in Tokarnia). Industrial heritage

Opatów. The Opatów Lament takes the form of a bronze plaque dating back to 1536, which is shown in part here. This forms an element of the Renaissance-style tomb of the Szydłowiecki family, as located in the Romanesque St. Martin's Church.

Bejsce. In St. Nicholas's Church, the Late Renaissance chapel with Mannerist-style sculpturework and the tomb of Elżbieta and Mikołaj Firlej.

of various ages is also present (a flint quarry in Krzemionki, primitive iron kilns in Nowa Słupia, and what is left of an early 19th-century ironworks in Samsonów). Other heritage attesting to the former wealth of the region takes the form of the ruins of the large Krzyżtopór Castle in Ujazd once famous for its affluence. Towering above Chęciny are the ruins of another castle for a while belonging to the Kings of Poland. The northern part of the voivodeship is in the Kielce-Sandomierz Upland, of which the highest part is taken by the Świętokrzyskie Mountains. This is a very attractive area for

Kurozwęki. A castle recalling Mediaeval times lost its defensive attributes to become a Baroque-style palace.

Krzemionki – a complex of Neolithic workings from which striped flint was mined for the purposes of tool-making.

Sandomierz. Beneath the Old Town streets there stretches a whole series of now-connected cellars that were constructed between the 13th and 16th centuries. In the past these served storage functions, but now they attract sightseers along this "Underground Tourist Trail" (Podziemna Trasa Turystyczna).

Sandomierz is a beautiful example of architectural and town planning. This photograph shows the Market Square with its Renaissance Town Hall.

tourists, full of interesting places, well-marked trails and mysterious caves (the "Paradise Cave" Jaskinia Raj is open to visitors). Nature is protected in the Świętokrzyski National Park, 9 Landscape Parks and a large number of other protected areas. There are also Monuments of Nature, of which the "Bartek" oak is Poland's most famous.

The southern part of the region in the Nida Trough is famous for the curative properties of its waters, and there are famous spas in Busko Zdrój and Solec Zdrój.

Ujazd – The Krzyżtopór Family castle. The Mannerist construction from the years 1627-1644 lay in ruins as early as in 1656 – having been put to the torch by the invading Swedes.

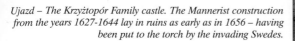

14 LUBELSKIE
VOIVODESHIP (LUBLIN)

Capital: **LUBLIN**

This eastern voivodeship covers more than 25,000 km², and takes in both the traditional Lublin region and parts once included within Małopolska, Mazowsze, Podlasie and Ruthenian Halicz (Chełm). Most of what is today included was already within the confines of Mieszko I's Poland. The seat of the voivodeship is Lublin, which has been in possession of its town charter since 1317. There was a defensive settlement of some significance here at least a century earlier, however, with the first traces of occupation going back to the 6th century. It was here in 1569 that the General Parliament was convened and the Lublin Union between Poland and Lithuania proclaimed. Lublin was already a major commercial and cultural centre at the time, though it was to fall later in the wars with Sweden. Renewed development on a major scale had to wait for the mid 19th century. The characteristic building is the Royal Castle with its Gothic Holy Trinity Chapel wherein the priceless Russo-Byzantine polychromy was funded by Władysław Jagiełło. A further major monument is the Old Town complex, with its Town Hall and wonderful churches set among picturesque tenement houses. The Second

Lublin. The Holy Trinity Chapel in the castle is Gothic in style, and preserves Russian-Byzantine polychromy from the early 15th century.

Lublin. The view from the Trinity Tower over the roofs of the Old Town, the Krakowska Gate, the Neo-Classical-style New Town Hall and the Church of the Holy Spirit.

Lublin. The Old Town Market Square, with the Neo-Gothic Trinity Tower in the background. Visitors may ascend to the viewing terrace, which is 40m above the ground.

World War saw the environs of the city blighted by the establishment of the Nazis' Majdanek Concentration Camp. The circa 360,000 people murdered there are remembered in a sombre monument, while the camp itself is a museum. The region's other larger centres are Zamość, Chełm, Biała Podlaska and Puławy, each boasting its own interesting history. Zamość is rather unique with its all-of-a-piece Renaissance plan, 17th-century Mannerist-Baroque Town Hall and Market Square set about with arcaded tenement houses – all the idea of Commander-in-Chief of the Army (Hetman) Jan Zamoyski from 1580, as well as the work of architect Bernardo Morando. Zamość Old

Janowiec. The attractive ruins of Mikołaj Firlej's 16th century castle by the Vistula.

Kazimierz Dolny is a picturesquely-located resort town above the Vistula, which boasts a Renaissance town plan. Here the view of Klasztorna Street, the Market Square and the Parish Church.

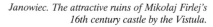

Gołąb. The elevation of the small House of the Sisters of Loreto, which dates back to 1640, features ceramic likenesses of the prophets in its niches, with this figure of Aaron for example present on the north side.

Puławy. The Palace of the Czartoryskis erected here in the 17th century and remodelled several times since. Here the Gothic Room which once served as the Chapel.

Wola Okrzejska. The single-storey wooden manor house from the early 19th century is the birthplace of Henryk Sienkiewicz. Today it is a museum devoted to the Nobel Prizewinning author.

Town was officially recognised as a UNESCO World Heritage Site in 1992. In turn, Chełm was the 13th-century capital of Ruthenian Halich, coming within Polish territory from 1366 on. Biała Podlaska was the property of the wealthy Radziwiłł family for 250 years from the mid 16th century onwards. Many surviving buildings and monuments from that time attest to the wealth of both family and town. The Academy opened here in 1628 was a higher education establishment which left Biała an important scientific and cultural

Kock. The mansion of the Jabłonowski family owes its elegant Neo-Classical form to a major rebuild carried out in the late 18th and early 19th centuries.

Kozłówka. Rebuilt in the Neo-Baroque style, the Zamoyski Palace has an impressive museum of interiors.

Lubartów. The 17th-century palace of the Sanguszko family stands in extensive parkland.

centre of Podlasie from the 17th century. Puławy is in turn best known for its palace and park, as is Kozłówka, a locality c. 40 km north of Lublin. No less interesting are the palaces and manors in Kock, Lubartów, Radzyń Podlaski and Rejowiec. In Zwierzyniec, an attraction in addition to the palace is the "Church on the water", while Nałęczów, which has been a well-known spa for years, boasts the Old Bath House. A particular place on the map of Poland is Kazimierz Dolny, a town of exceptional atmosphere and charm. The market square is surrounded by Renaissance-style tenement houses overlooked from on high by the ruins of a castle with a 14th-century Gothic tower. Hardly surprising that this is a mecca for artists. The places of worship of a number

Leśna Podlaska has a Paulite monastery complex and Sanctuary to the Virgin Mary. The Chapel has a well regarded as miraculous.

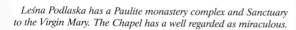

Uchanie. The 8-metre-high tomb of Anna Uchańska and Paweł Uchański in the Church of the Assumption. This is a work of Pińczów stone and alabaster produced by Tomasz Nikiel, who took on Santi Gucci's old workshop.

Kodeń. The Late-Renaissance St. Anne's Church is a sanctuary with a miraculous likeness of the Mother of God known as the Queen and Mother of Podlasie.

Kostomłoty is a village featuring the world's only community of Byzantine-Slavic Rite Catholics. The wooden place of worship is St. Nikita's Church.

of different faiths can be found in the region: Catholic churches, Orthodox churches – especially in the eastern part – and synagogues in such places as Szczebrzeszyn, Włodawa and Zamość. Nature in this region has been brought under protection inter alia in two National Parks centred on the Polesie marshlands and Roztocze Hills, as well as in numerous Landscape Parks and Nature Reserves.

As the tongue-twisting verse by Jan Brzechwa had it "W Szczebrzeszynie chrząszcz brzmi w trzcinie i Szczebrzeszyn z tego słynie" ("In Szczebrzeszyn, the beetle can be heard in the reeds, and that is what Szczebrzeszyn is famous for"). The insect now has a statue in its honour located in front of the Town Hall.

The Bug. This picturesque and unregulated river is a tributary
of the Vistula. It forms Poland's eastern border along a significant
part of its length.

Zamość, known as the "Padua of the North", was designed by
Italian architect Bernardo Morando. The panorama of the Old
Town in Zamość, the view of the Town Hall and the Armenian
quarter from the cathedral tower.

Zamość. The two-storey arcaded tenement houses on the Large
Market Square (Rynek Wielki) recall Italian architecture.

15 PODKARPACKIE
VOIVODESHIP

Capital: **RZESZÓW**

Lying in the south-eastern corner of Poland, this voivodeship borders with Ukraine to the east and Slovakia to the south. Industrialisation has been limited here, though sulphur is mined near Tarnobrzeg, while deposits of natural gas are also present. Considerable parts of the voivodeship are taken by the Eastern Beskids and Bieszczady Mountains, as well as the Low Beskids and Beskid Foreland. Abandoned by many of its inhabitants after the War, the wild Bieszczady Mountains earn many admirers with their unspoilt nature and limited numbers of visitors. Well-prepared trails for walkers and tracks for mountain bikers and skiers can be enjoyed in peace here. The mountain views can also be taken in from a horse's back and the visitor can even partake in a cowbowy-like cattle roundup. A National Park was established in the Bieszczady in 1973, and this now covers 27,800 ha. It also forms part of the Eastern Carpathians International Biosphere Reserve, along with adjacent protected areas in Ukraine and Slovakia. The voivodeship also boasts the greater part of the Magurski (Magura) NP, which includes the most precious parts of the Low Beskids. Several Landscape Parks and a host of Nature

Rzeszów is a town on the Wisłok. Here the Market Square with its Eclectic 19th-century Town Hall and Monument to Tadeusz Kościuszko.

Rzeszów. The Lubomirski's castle is a 19th-century building atop 17th-century fortifications.

Leżajsk. The famous organ from 1680-1693 is one of Poland's finest. Richly carved, it stands in the Church of the Annunciation.

Baranów Sandomierski. The arcaded courtyard of the 16th-17th century Mannerist castle.

Reserves complete the lineup of protected areas. The region retains populations of various faiths and origins: there are Poles, Lemko people and Ukrainians – hence the presence here of many Russian Orthodox and Greek Catholic churches, as well as Roman Catholic ones. Eight Polish and eight Ukrainian wooden Orthodox churches in the Carpathian region have now been entered on UNESCO's World Heritage List. There were many Jews here too, before the War, but all that tells of their presence now are old cemeteries and synagogues. The capital of the Podkarpackie voivodeship is Rzeszów – a city founded in 1354 on the site of an old fortified township from the Middle Ages. From 1772 on, the city was in the part of the country partitioned off by Austria, only

Łańcut. The beautiful 17th-century park has a two-storey castle remodelled in the French neo-Baroque style.

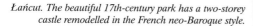

Chotyniec, the church of the Nativity of the Blessed Virgin Mary, built about 1600. The framework construction of the building's structure is clearly visible.

returning to Poland in 1918. The most important piece of architectural heritage in Rzeszów is the Bernardine Church of the Assumption from the first half of the 17th century. The province's very interesting second city is Przemyśl, which was a township as early as in the 10th century, having probably been settled first in the 2nd century B.C. In the scond half of the 19th century A.D., the city took on a formidable appearance as towers and forts were erected. Nevertheless, much old construction remains, especially in the Old Town with its 15th-16th century cathedral, remodelled in the Baroque style. Fine castles may also be visited

Przemyśl-Bakończyce. Prince Hieronim Lubomirski had his Eclectic palace put up here, taking building material from the walls of the old 17th-century castle.

Przemyśl is a city of many cultures. A Baroque-style iconostasis is to be seen in the former Jesuit Church handed over to the Greek-Catholic faith in 1991.

Krasiczyn. The Renaissance-Mannerist Castle of the Krasickis in a park from the 19th century.

The Western Bieszczady Mountains. The renowned and much-visited massif of Połonina Wetlińska, which peaks at 1255m Roh.

Posada Rybotycka. The defensible Church of St. Onuphrius is the oldest surviving Orthodox Church anywhere in the Polish lands, dating back to the 14th-16th centuries. It comprises three interlinked towers.

at Krasiczyn, Łańcut and Baranów Sandomierski. Krasiczyn is around 10 km west of Przemyśl. Its imposing Renaissance-Mannerist style castle set in landscaped parkland is one of Poland's most beautiful and was built in stages between 1592 and 1618. Of a rather different character is Łańcut Castle, a splendid magnate's residence from the 17th century which currently presents its Neo-Baroque French style. The old coach-house building now houses the Museum of Horse-drawn Transport. Łańcut is famous for its festival of serious music. Another Museum – of Interiors (mainly from the 16th and 17th centuries), and Poland's

Kalwaria Pacławska, an 18th century Franciscan monastic complex. Church interiors.

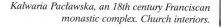

Radruż. An Orthodox church and freestanding bell tower seen from the west, with one of the two adjoining cemeteries.

Haczów. "The Coronation of the Mother of God" is polychromy dating back to 1494 and still preserved in the chancel of what is the largest Gothic church in wood, and also one of the oldest (not only in Poland).

In Magurski National Park, a picturesque waterfall spills over the sandstone outcrops.

only sulphur museum are to be found in Baranów Sandomierski in a castle dating back to the years 1591-1606. Romantics and lovers of antiquities should stop of at Sieniawa, in an unusual hotel formed from a beautiful Baroque palace surrounded by parkland, which was laid out in the late 17th and early 18th centuries. In Leżajsk, the Bernardine church has one of Poland's finest and most famous organs, which forms the centrepiece of the town's international festivals of organ music. Bóbrka is also worth a visit, as a cradle of the world's oil industry. The Ignacy Łukasiewicz Open Air Museum takes its name from the discoverer of the oil refining process and inventor of the oil lamp.

The place of the former Radocyna village, liquidated during the "Vistula" action, serves as a spot for making charcoal.

16 MAŁOPOLSKIE
VOIVODESHIP

Capital: **KRAKÓW**

This voivodeship takes in an area very diverse from the points of view of relief, industrialisation, tradition and folklore. The present-day administrative boundaries correspond quite closely with those of the historical Małopolska ("Little Poland"), regarded as one of the core areas of Polish statehood, and encompassing the Małopolska Upland, as well as most Polish parts of the Carpathians, and the Sandomierz and Oświęcim Depressions (Sandomierz itself is now within Świętokrzyskie voivodeship). It is through this region that trading routes from Western Europe through to the Black Sea ran, and this favoured the development and enrichment of the area, as did mining for salt and metal ores. The seat of today's voivodeship and the Małopolska of old is Kraków, a city that was already of major political significance by the end of the 10th century. A Bishopric was created here in the year 1000, and the first Cathedral erected on the Wawel Hill. Though city status was not in fact obtained until 1257, Kraków had been the preferred residence of the monarchs from the mid 11th century on. It became the official capital in 1320, when Władysław Łokietek ("the Short") was

Kraków. The Main Market Square with the Gothic St. Mary's Church.

Kraków. In St. Mary's Church, one of the scenes on Veit Stoss Gothic altar of 1477-1489 portrays the "Descent of the Holy Ghost".

Kraków, The Wawel Cathedral of Sts. Wacław and Stanisław the Bishop. The characteristic domes are of the Waza and Zygmuntowska Chapels.

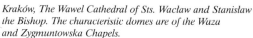

View of Szeroka Street in the Kazimierz district, a reminder of old times when most of the inhabitants here were Jewish. Wooden signs above modest shops – this is what a poorer district of the city looked like.

The Benedictine Abbey in Tyniec, which is now a district of Cracow. It was in the 11th century that work began on this building on limestone heights by the Vistula.

crowned in the Wawel Cathedral. Forty-four years later, King Kazimierz the Great founded the Krakow Academy – Poland's first higher education establishment. The period of real flowering of the city continued until the end of the 16th century, with culture, architecture, all forms of art and learning flourishing. Many foreign artists and teachers came here to live. However, the transfer of the royal residence to Warsaw in the late 16th and early 17th centuries marked the onset of a slow but sure decline of Kraków, even if this

Rudno. The ruins of the 14th-century Knights' Castle in Tenczyn.

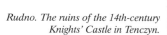

The Prądnik Valley includes the sharply-incised Stodoliska Canyon, as just one fine example of this area's very diverse karst relief.

Jaskinia Ciemna (the "Dark Cave") in Ojcowski National Park. The main chamber is 90 m long. Altogether the Park boasts around 700 caves and other rocky hollows.

was still the place of coronation and royal burial. World War II left the city relatively intact in the material sense – its architectural heritage remained in place. However, the people which made the city so special were not spared, as the Nazis murdered all the professors and scientific employees in higher education. Today, while Warsaw is undoubtedly the capital, it is still for many Kraków that is the country's most important cultural and educational centre. It also represents the most important complex of monuments, entered on the World Heritage List run by UNESCO. A further curiosity, also a World Heritage Site, is the Wieliczka

The Church and Barefoot Carmelite Monastery in Czerna, north of Krzeszowice. It was funded in 1625 by Agnieszka Firlejowa.

Pieskowa Skała. One of Poland's largest castles from the age of chivalry.

Korzkiew. A 14th-century knights' castle is located here, and forms part of the "Eagles' Nests" Trail (Szlak Orlich Gniazd) – along with other fortresses from the Middle Ages stretching between Częstochowa and Kraków).

Auschwitz I. The Concentration and Extermination Camp dating back to the times of World War II, a place of death and martyrdom for several million human beings, and now a museum and most potent symbol of the Holocaust.

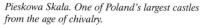

Salt Mine, with its beautiful chambers, sculptures and even chandeliers carved out of the rock salt. The Chapel of St. Kinga is perhaps the finest chamber of all, while the mine also operates a sanatorium for respiratory and rheumatic diseases some 200 m below the surface. In a well-preserved state and usually open to visitors are the castles in Niepołomice, Niedzica, Nowy Wiśnicz, Pieskowa Skała and Sucha Beskidzka. Szymbark in turn has a quite unsual fortified manor. Many of the towns

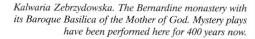

Kalwaria Zebrzydowska. The Bernardine monastery with its Baroque Basilica of the Mother of God. Mystery plays have been performed here for 400 years now.

Niepołomice – the Renaissance-style royal hunting palace with its cloistered courtyard.

St Kinga's Chapel in Wieliczka is situated 100 m below ground – it is the most impressive and opulent of the mine's chambers.

Nowy Wiśnicz. The castle is a Baroque-styled fortified residence with corner towers and surrounding bastions.

of Małopolska also retain their original urban plan plus many old buildings. Examples here might be Nowy Sącz, Tarnów and Stary Sącz. Many interesting contemporary buildings are also to be seen up and down the region, including the painted wooden architecture typical of Podhale, as exemplified in such villages as Zalipie. A must-see of a quite different kind more likely to generate reflection, deep sadness or even horror is the museum on the site of the former Nazi extermination camp of Auschwitz-Birkenau in Oświęcim. However, it is not merely history and buildings that make this the most-visited

At Tokarnia near Cracow, the Palm Sunday congregation parades a wooden figure of Christ on a donkey through the streets.

Szymbark. The fortified mansion of the Gładysz family, built in the 16th century, is now part of an open-air ethnographic museum.

part of Poland. The Tatra, Pieniny and Beskidy Mountains are all here, plus the Kraków-Częstochowa Upland, and hence a wealth of nature protected in 6 National Parks. The Tatra Mountains draw fans of alpine tourism, climbing and winter sports, while the area's National Park combines with the adjacent Park in Slovakia to form an International Biosphere Reserve. Nearby Zakopane is Poland's "winter capital", combining with other localities in Podhale to offer a fine accommodation base. Skiers are otherwise well provided for by the large number of lifts and runs. The Pieniny

The arcade along the bottom of late 16th-century tenement house lining the Market Square in Tarnów. The interconnected buildings provide the seat of the District Museum.

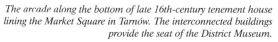
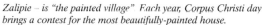

Zalipie – is "the painted village" Each year, Corpus Christi day brings a contest for the most beautifully-painted house.

Binarowa. The chancel walls of the church are decorated with a series of scenes of the Passion. The baroque-style altar features a sculpture of the Madonna and Child, part of a 15th-century Gothic triptych.

The Church of the Protection of the Mother of God in Owczary. The mixture of slender towers and multi-angled roofs covered with wooden shingles and also the beautiful surroundings in which they are located make these works of sacred architecture uniquely beautiful.

Dębno – the 15 th century wooden church of St. Michael.

Ludźmierz is regarded as the oldest village in the Podhale region (from the early 13th century) – it is famous for its miraculous likeness of the Mother of God.

Mountains are in turn renowned for the picturesque gorge of the Dunajec, in which organized rafting trips allow visitors to enjoy the scenery at close quarter. The Pieniński National Park was founded here, while the region's other National Parks centre on Mt. Babia Góra and the Gorce Mountains, as well the Magura Hills (shared with the Podkarpackie voivodeship) and the Ojców Hills, where fine examples of the limestone

The Dunajec Gorge within the Pieniny Mountains National Park, as seen from Mt. Sokolica.

Łopuszna. The wooden manor of the Tetmajer
family now houses the Museum of the Nobility.

Niedzica. The Gothic-Renaissance fortress
as seen from the dam on the Dunajec.

The royal castle in Czorsztyn guarded for centuries the merchant
route running along the Valley of Dunajec to Hungary.
When the waters rise, the castle is reflected in the glassy
surface of Lake Czorsztyńskie.

Zakopane. Towering above the town
is the characteristic outline of Giewont.

Zakopane. The chapel in Jaszczurówka, built in 1908, was designed in the so-called Zakopiański style by Stanisław Witkiewicz.

Podhale. A colourful Corpus Christi procession.

Willa Pod Jedlami, designed by Stanisław Witkiewicz (1897), is recognized as a model example of the Zakopane style.

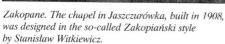

landscape of the Kraków-Częstochowa Upland are protected. A particular attraction of the Ojcowski NP are its more than 200 caves. Eighteen localities in Małopolska have spa or health-resort status, with the most popular places to take a cure being Rabka, Krynica, Szczawnica and Muszyna. There are also two important Catholic sanctuaries Kalwaria Zebrzydowska, and the nearby Wadowice, birthplace of Karol Wojtyła – better known as Pope John Paul II.

Zakopane. Poland's most famous pedestrianised promenade is Krupówki Street in Zakopane, the heart of the town and a "must-do" for visitors.

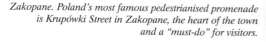

The Tatra Mountains. The Gąsienicowa Valley, with a view on to the snowy summits of Granaty, Kozi Wierch, Zamarła Turnia and Kościelec.

The High Tatras. The Siklawa Falls (c. 40 m high) are the most powerful and beautiful in the Tatras, and are situated at the upper end of the Roztoki Valley.

The High Tatras. The area around the Morskie Oko ("Eye of the Sea") Tarn, with the peaks along the Rybiego Potoku Valley known as Mięguszowiecki, Cubryna and Mnich (the characteristic "Monk").

The Western Tatars. Accessible to tourists, the Mylna Cave cuts into the impressive rock massif of Raptawicka Turnia.

The Tatra Mountains. Rather resembling goats, chamois are classed in a separate family. They enjoy legal protection.

POLAND

CHRISTIAN PARMA
photography

RENATA GRUNWALD-KOPEĆ
text

BOGNA PARMA
layout, captions to photographs, editor

JAMES R.A. RICHARDS
translation

Wydawnictwo PARMA PRESS
ELIZA DZIENIO
dtp

Wydawnictwo PARMA PRESS
05 270 Marki, al. Józefa Piłsudskiego 189 b
+48 22/781 16 48, 781 16 49
e-mail: wydawnictwo@parmapress.com.pl
www.parmapress.com.pl

ISBN 978-83-7777-175-4